AMELIA EARHART
FLYING SOLO

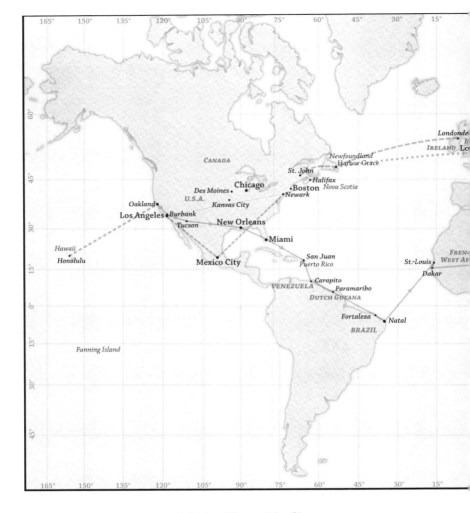

Aviation History Timeline

1903	Wilbur and Orville Wright make the first controlled flight in a heavier-than-air airplane. Their plane travelled 850 feet.
1909	Louis Blériot made the first flight across the English Channel. The flight took 37 minutes.
1914	World War I saw the first use of airplanes in wartime.
1919	Capt. John Alcock and Lt. Arthur Whitten Brown completed the first successful non-stop Atlantic crossing from Newfoundland to Ireland in 16 hours.
1926	Richard Byrd and Floyd Bennet made the first flight over the North Pole.
1927	Charles Lindbergh flies *The Spirit of St. Louis* across the Atlantic Ocean non-stop from New York to Paris in the first solo translatlantic flight.
1928	Amelia Earhart becomes the first woman to fly across the Atlantic Ocean.
1932	Amelia Earhart flies solo across the Atlantic Ocean.
1933	Wiley Post is the first to fly solo around the world.
1935	Amelia Earhart is the first to fly solo from Hawaii to Oakland, California.

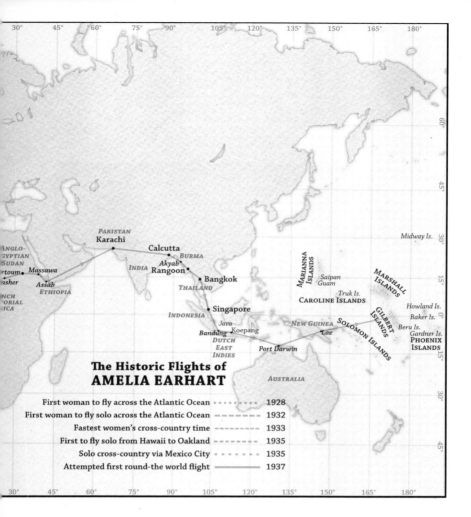

The Historic Flights of AMELIA EARHART

First woman to fly across the Atlantic Ocean · · · · · · · · 1928
First woman to fly solo across the Atlantic Ocean — — — — 1932
Fastest women's cross-country time - - - - - - - - - 1933
First to fly solo from Hawaii to Oakland - - - - - - - - 1935
Solo cross-country via Mexico City · · · · · · · 1935
Attempted first round-the world flight ——————— 1937

1937   Amelia Earhart and Fred Noonan disappear on a flight from New Guinea to Howland Island on their way around the world.

1947   Chuck Yeager breaks the sound barrier aboard a rocket-powered Bell X-1 plane.

1949   B-50 Superfortress, *Lucky Lady II*, completes the first non-stop around-the-world flight.

1957   Sputnik I, the first satellite to orbit the earth, is launched.

1958   Pan American Airlines begins the first commercial transatlantic jet service.

1961   Yuri Gagarin becomes the first man in space aboard the *Vostok I*, orbiting the earth every 108 minutes.

1969   Neil Armstrong becomes the first man to set foot on the moon. The spacecraft, *Apollo 11*, manned by Armstrong, Buzz Aldrin, and Michael Collins, was launched from earth on July 16th and returned on July 24th.

1976   The Concorde makes the first supersonic commercial passenger flight across the Atlantic Ocean.

1981   The first space shuttle, *Columbia*, is launched.

1989   Bryan Allen flies the *Gossamer Albatross* across the English Channel using pedal power.

Amelia Earhart

AMELIA EARHART

JOHN BURKE

STERLING PUBLISHING CO., INC.
New York

A FLYING POINT PRESS BOOK

Design: PlutoMedia
Front cover photograph: Corbis
Frontispiece: The Granger Collection, New York

Library of Congress Cataloging-in-Publication Data

Burke, John, 1915-1975.
Amelia Earhart : flying solo / John Burke.
p. cm. — (Sterling point books)
Abridged ed. of: Winged legend. c1970.
Includes bibliographical references and index.
ISBN-13: 978-1-4027-4520-1 (trade)
ISBN-10: 1-4027-4520-6
ISBN-13: 978-1-4027- 4140-1 (pbk.)
ISBN-10: 1-4027- 4140-5
1. Earhart, Amelia, 1897-1937. 2. Women air pilots—United States—Biography.
3. Air pilots—United States—Biography. I. Burke, John, 1915-1975.
Winged legend. II. Title. III. Title: Flying solo.

TL540.E3B872 2007
629.13092—dc22
[B]
                                    2006032132

2   4   6   8   10   9   7   5   3

Published by Sterling Publishing Co., Inc.
387 Park Avenue South, New York, NY 10016
Abridged from the book originally published by G. P. Putnam's Sons under the title *Winged Legend: The Story of Amelia Earhart*
Copyright © 1970 by John Burke
New material in this updated edition
Copyright © 2007 by Flying Point Press
Map copyright © by Richard Thompson, Creative Freelancers, Inc.
Distributed in Canada by Sterling Publishing
c/o Canadian Manda Group, 165 Dufferin Street
Toronto, Ontario, Canada M6K 3H6
Distributed in the United Kingdom by GMC Distribution Services
Castle Place, 166 High Street, Lewes, East Sussex, England BN7 IXU
Distributed in Australia by Capricorn Link (Australia) Pty. Ltd.
P.O. Box 704, Windsor, NSW 2756, Australia

Sterling ISBN-13: 978-1-4027-4140-1
ISBN-10: 1-4027-4140-5

For information about custom editions, special sales, premium and corporate purchases, please
contact Sterling Special Sales Department at 800-805-5489 or specialsales@sterlingpub.com.

CONTENTS

CONTENTS

AMELIA EARHART
FLYING SOLO

CHAPTER I

"THE GIRL IN BROWN, WHO WALKS ALONE"

AMELIA EARHART'S FIRST GLIMPSE OF A genuine airplane, or "aeroplane" as it was then spelled, came one summer's day when her father took the family to the Iowa State Fair in Des Moines. Aviation then was in its first toddling stages, and the first aircraft were rickety affairs of wood and wire and oiled canvas, powered by tiny sputtering engines. "Flights" were a matter of a few miles, often terminated by engine failures and forced landings among the cornstalks.

Mr. Earhart watched impatiently while Amelia and her younger sister Muriel indulged themselves in the merry-go-round, the pony rides, and buying paper hats. He was eager for his first look at a plane; it had been only a few years since Wilbur and Orville Wright faltered into the sky over the sand dunes of Kitty Hawk.

Finally their father managed to round up his family and escort them over to the flying field on the edge of the fairgrounds. Amelia, though uninterested, would remember later her first sight of the machine which some twenty years later would make her a world celebrity and engage her whole life. It was an unimpressive contraption, as she would recall: a biplane with the pilot, his face masked by goggles, sitting with his feet on the crossbars, the engine and a big wooden propeller behind him. The engine coughed. Ungainly as a gooney bird, the craft trundled along the rough surface of the pasture; its rusty ailerons creaked, and suddenly it floundered into the air.

Edwin Earhart was transfixed by the miracle of man-made flight and tried to interest his daughters in the spectacle. But Amelia could not be distracted from fussing with her paper hat and wondered aloud when they could return to the merry-go-round. So much for first impressions. . . .

Amelia and Muriel were adventuresome girls. At their grandparents' home in Atchison, Kansas, they had built their own rickety roller coaster. With the help of their young uncle, Carl Otis, they constructed a shaky trestle from the roof of their father's toolshed. The test pilot, naturally, was Amelia, who was growing up to be a towheaded tomboy. The little cart she occupied while it hurtled down the track ended up running off the trestle and dumping its passenger. Amelia dusted herself off after her first crash landing, and the girls' mother, attracted to the scene by the sounds of the small disaster and Muriel's wails, put an end to any further experiments with the roller coaster. About the same time, of course, a whole generation of pioneer fliers was endangering its young limbs by jumping off barn roofs with umbrella parachutes or building kites strong enough to bear a boy aloft; so Amelia Earhart was well within a tradition waiting to be born.

Sadly, the girls' childhood was tinged with hardship. On the doorstep to middle age, Edwin Earhart had suddenly discovered the joys of alcohol. Suddenly and with shattering impact, the melodrama of alcoholism intruded upon the lives of his wife and daughters.

There was nothing carefree about the rest of Amelia Earhart's girlhood. Every evening she and her mother and sister would wait anxiously for her father's return, listening for his footsteps to determine whether or not he had been drinking. Nothing seemed to work out for the family.

It soon became clear that Edwin Earhart could no longer be relied on as a breadwinner; the family would have become objects of public charity if it hadn't been for the income from Mrs. Earhart's trust fund. There seemed to be no alternative but to break up the family temporarily. The Shedd family, whom the Earharts had known in Des Moines, had moved to Chicago and invited Mrs. Earhart and her daughters to stay with them as long as they wanted. Meanwhile, Earhart would go to Kansas City, live with his sister and her family, and open a law office.

Mrs. Earhart and the girls journeyed to Chicago and moved in with the Shedds. Apparently the recent years of anxiety, shame, bewilderment, and sheer bad luck had not crushed Amelia's spirit. She was intent on getting through school on schedule and finding some way of helping her father. Quite possibly she felt more sympathy for him than for her mother; she could not despise him for being defeated by circumstances, even though many of them were self-inflicted.

Amelia was determined to get the best possible grounding in scientific subjects. The nearest high school was Morgan Park High, which her sister attended. Amelia, however, refused to enroll until she had inspected the chemistry laboratory. "It was just a kitchen sink," she declared, refusing to attend the school. She then interviewed the principals of several other high schools and found their facilities inadequate for her senior year, which might, for all she knew, be the end of her formal education. Finally she settled on Hyde Park High School because it offered adequate courses in chemistry and physics.

Amelia was a serious student who demanded and received permission to spend the English period in the school library. She read four times the number of required books for the course. The caption under her picture in the yearbook for the graduating class of 1916 was singularly apt: "The girl in brown, who walks alone."

CHAPTER 2

NURSING THE WAR WOUNDED

THE SUMMER OF AMELIA'S GRADUATION, SHE and her mother and sister moved back to Kansas City. Against considerable odds, it appeared that Edwin Earhart had found his footing. Alcohol was never a serious problem again, though by then the damage to his marriage, if not to his relations with his daughters, was probably irreparable. He was practicing law again, and that was all to the good.

He had found a small house, and the family was reunited. Another threat to the Earhart girls' future education, however, loomed. Mrs. Earhart learned that her brother, Mark Otis, had been unwise in acting as guardian of her trust fund from their grandparents' estate.

Waiting for that issue to be settled, Amelia stayed out of school until funds were more available for furthering her education. She entered prep school in Pennsylvania and planned to attend Bryn Mawr, but it soon developed that Amelia was not quite the Ivy League type.

Socially, she was still the nonconformist, the odd girl out. She was invited to join one of the three secret sororities and enjoyed being a member until she learned that some of the girls at the school were excluded from joining any of the secret societies. Her efforts to persuade her own sorority to take in more members, anyone who wanted to join, were met with failure, so she carried her case to the headmistress.

"Every girl," she said, "ought to have the fun of belonging to a sorority if she wants to."

For her Christmas vacation in 1917, Amelia journeyed to Toronto to visit her sister, who was attending St. Margaret's College there. As a believer in direct action, she experienced another change of course during those dreary winter weeks. World War I was then entering its climactic phase, and the base hospitals of Toronto were jammed with casualties from the Western Front. "There for the first time," she later wrote, "I realized what the World War meant. Instead of new uniforms and brass bands, I saw the results of four years' desperate struggle; men without arms and legs, men who were paralyzed and men who were blind."

"I'd like to stay here and help in the hospitals," she wrote her mother. "I can't bear the thought of going back to school and being so useless."

After taking a crash course in Red Cross First Aid and enlisting in the Voluntary Aid Detachment, she was assigned to the Spadina Military Hospital and became a nurse's aide. Her own account of her duties was modest and understated. "Nurse's aides," she later recalled, "did everything from scrubbing floors to playing tennis with convalescing patients. The patients called us 'sister' and we hotfooted here and there to attend their wants. 'Please rub my back, sister. I'm so tired lying in bed.' Or, 'Won't you bring me ice cream today instead of rice pudding?'

"We were on duty from seven in the morning until seven at night with two hours off in the afternoon. I spent a great deal of time in the diet kitchen and later in the dispensary, because I knew a little chemistry."

Saturday afternoons she and Muriel went riding on horses rented from a stable near the fairgrounds. Often they rode with Canadian Army and Flying Corps officers, who were stationed nearby. It was during that winter of 1917–18 that her interest in aviation was awakened.

One of her riding companions was a Captain Spaulding of the Royal Flying Corps, who admired Amelia's Western style of horsemanship and the way she managed a half-broken horse which had once belonged to a cavalry colonel. "Watching the way you ride that horse reminds me of the way I have to fly my plane," Captain Spaulding told her. "Sometimes she goes along smooth as silk and then she gets contrary and bucks a bit just to show off."

He then invited the girls to come out to the airfield and watch him fly. They eagerly accepted but were disappointed when Spaulding cited regulations that forbade him to take them up for a ride. Soon Amelia was spending most of her off-duty hours at the airdrome watching the training maneuvers. "I remember the sting of the snow on my face," she later wrote, "as it was blown back from the propellers when the training planes took off on skis."

The planes were mostly Curtiss Jennies, Canadian Royal Flying Corps trainers, but when they were piloted skillfully, the grace and speed of their flight held Amelia enthralled. Flying had captured her imagination long before she went up for her first flight. There was a poetry about those tiny sputtering machines, struggling into the air against the harsh northerly winds, that utterly fascinated her.

They made almost as great an impression on her as the suffering she witnessed in the wards of the base hospital.

That imprint of endless agony, of wasted and shattered youth, would never leave her mind. In later years she would be staunchly antiwar, not only as a matter of intellectual conviction but because she could not forget the suffering she had seen at Spadina hospital.

She stayed on for almost a year as a nurse's aide, until after the Armistice, November 11, 1918. Working almost around the clock, with only a few hours' sleep snatched at odd intervals, finally caught up with her. She came down with a serious attack of pneumonia. When she had recovered sufficiently to travel, she joined Muriel in Northampton, Massachusetts, where her sister was attending Smith College. Amelia was too restless to dedicate herself wholeheartedly to convalescence and relieved the boredom by taking a course in automobile engine repair, not then regarded as a feminine pursuit. It did not appeal to her as a career, but she felt it might come in handy, somehow.

Her current ambition was to take up a medical career, an interest awakened by her year as a nurse's aide. After a summer spent resting on the shores of Lake George with her sister and mother, she entered Columbia University in New York as a premedical student. Characteristically, she overloaded herself with work. In addition to a full schedule of laboratory and lecture courses at Columbia and its sister school, Barnard, she enrolled as an auditor in other classes.

She also subjected herself to a rigorous self-examination during that year at Columbia and came up with the conclusion that she really wasn't cut out to be a doctor. She was still taking compass bearings on what she really wanted to do with her life.

She also withdrew from Columbia because domestic storm signals were flying from the Los Angeles home of her parents. They wrote rather urgently asking her to continue her education in California. Obviously what they wanted was a buffer. Amelia did not much care for the role but told Muriel that she would go home and see if she could keep their parents together. After that, she told Muriel, "I'm going to come back here and live my life."

CHAPTER 3

FLEDGLING

AMELIA WENT OUT TO CALIFORNIA IN THE summer of 1920. By this time Amelia had acquired an overriding interest in aviation. It had fascinated her ever since she had watched the training activities at the RFC field outside Toronto. It became almost an obsession after her father took her to an air show at Long Beach, when she discovered how much it cost to learn to fly: one thousand dollars. A short time later she went up for the first time from a suburban airfield out on Wilshire Boulevard hemmed in by oil derricks. The pilot was Frank Hawks, who was to hold many speed records.

Amelia immediately signed up for flying lessons. The family budget could not afford that expense, so she took a job at the Los Angeles telephone company. Her instructor was Neta Snook, the first woman to graduate from the Curtiss School of Aviation; later she took more advanced lessons from John Montijo, a former Army instructor (the Air Force was then part of the Signal Corps).

For the first time in her life Amelia felt really free, alive, in her proper element. Airborne, even in one of the rickety trainers then in use, most of them Army surplus, she felt entirely secure, the problems of her earthbound life temporarily eliminated. "From then on," she would recall, "the family scarcely saw me for I worked all week and spent what I had of Saturday and Sunday at the airport a few miles from the town. The trip there took more than an hour to the end of the carline, and then a walk of several miles along the dusty highway. In those days it was really necessary for a woman to wear breeches and a leather coat. The fields were dusty and the planes hard to climb into. Flyers dressed the part in semi-military outfits and in order to be as inconspicuous as possible, I fell into the same style." She also cropped her hair. Inconspicuous or not, she loved the costume, reveled in the atmosphere of a dusty airfield with its ramshackle hangars and the wind sock which passed for meteorological expertise.

With an instructor in the rear cockpit ready to grab the controls, she practiced the various aerial maneuvers, takeoffs, and landings in a Curtiss Canuck, a descendant of the wartime Jenny trainer. What seemed to be "stunting" to those on the ground actually, as she later explained, was learning how to cope with emergencies that arose in flight. "The fundamental stunts taught to students are slips, stalls and spins. . . . Loops, barrel rolls and variations and combinations of many kinds are included depending on the instruction desired. . . . A knowledge of some stunts is judged necessary to good flying. Unless a pilot has actually recovered from a stall, has actually put his plane into a spin and brought it out, he cannot know accurately what those acts entail. He should be familiar enough with abnormal positions of his craft to recover without having to think how."

The hazards of stunting admittedly were part of the joy of flying to Amelia Earhart. Perhaps this was because of what veteran pilots observed of her from her first fledgling flights: She was a "natural," the aircraft became an extension of herself, she was coolheaded, and she handled a plane with the same sure, steady hands with which she managed an unruly horse.

Stunting was often merely showing off for the groundlings, but she admitted she had fun performing the barrel rolls, sideslips, Immelmann turns, and other aerial acrobatics. "So much so, in fact, I have sometimes thought that transport companies would do well to have a 'recreation plane' for their pilots who don't have any chance to play in the big transports or while on duty. If a little stunt ship were available, the men could go up 5,000 feet and 'turn it inside out' to relieve the monotony of hours of straight flying."

The exhilaration of soaring into the still smog-free skies over Los Angeles was so great that Amelia could hardly bear coming back to earth. Once she jumped out of her training plane and exclaimed to her sister Muriel, "It's so breathtakingly beautiful up there, I want to fly whenever I can."

Muriel was more earthbound and was not tempted to join in the sport but often went out to the field on Wilshire Boulevard, where the adobe dust rose in clouds whenever there was a takeoff, with a picnic basket for Amelia and her friends. The pilots and mechanics, many of them veterans of the Allied Expeditionary Force or other World War I air forces, were a rough and ready group, profane and hardbitten, but they moderated their language and conduct when the Earhart girls were around.

The only irksome thing was that it took Amelia so many months to earn enough money at the telephone company to pay for enough lessons before she was ready to solo.

When the big day arrived, she was cool and self-confident. Clad in breeches, boots, and a long leather jacket, with the traditional scarf around her neck, she vaulted into the cockpit of a Kinner biplane; a mechanic spun the prop, and she zoomed down the runway with the nonchalance of a veteran. She was on her own now; there was no one to seize the controls if anything went wrong. Such possibilities did not concern her, except as a challenge to be joyfully met. Early in her training, when Neta Snook was her instructor, their Canuck had suffered an engine failure shortly after takeoff. Miss Snook made an emergency landing in a nearby cabbage field. Amelia was so self-possessed that she reached over and cut the switch before the plane touched down.

On her solo flight Amelia took the biplane up to 5,000 feet, maneuvered it expertly for a while, and then came down to make what she later admitted was "an exceptionally poor landing." Most beginners stayed up until their gasoline supply was almost exhausted out of fear of making their first solo landing.

When she jumped out of the plane, a pilot who had been watching told her, "You didn't do anything right but land rottenly." For a student pilot, he meant. "Don't you know you're supposed to be so ground-shy you stay up until the gas tank runs dry?"

Her parents, though mildly disapproving, were certainly indulgent toward their eldest daughter's obsession with airplanes. They did not flinch too much even after Amelia walked away from two crash landings. Once she had to pancake her plane in a farmer's field during a rainstorm; the plane nosed over on its back, and Amelia hung upside down from her safety belt. Another time she was forced down into a field overgrown with high weeds. Again the plane flipped over, but this time Amelia's safety belt broke, and she was flung out of the cockpit. Neither of the accidents resulted from recklessness or incompetence; they were all part of the hazard of flying in the day of put-put engines not much bigger than a motorcycle's.

At considerable sacrifice, her parents and sister chipped in to buy her a plane on her twenty-fourth birthday, July 24, 1922. It was a Kinner Canary—a small yellow biplane fabricated by William Kinner, a pioneer aircraft designer and a friend of hers at the Wilshire Boulevard airfield. Most of the money for that present came from her mother, out of her share of the proceeds from the recent sale of her parents' house in Kansas. Apparently Amelia's close-knit family recognized, or sensed, that flying was going to be more than a hobby with her.

From the few books then available on the subject, from

old newspapers and other sources, she began researching the brief but lively history of women in aviation, going back to the lighter-than-air days. Somewhere she acquired a handbill advertising the balloon ascent of Mrs. Graham, "the only female aeronaut," from the Royal Gardens, London, on July 11, 1850. She learned that while the public knew all about the pioneering exploits of the Wright brothers, there was also a Wright sister, Katherine, who turned over her salary as a teacher to her brothers, Orville and Wilbur, to allow them to continue their experiments. "Much of our effort has been inspired by her," one of them said.

So far as Amelia could learn from the records, the first woman to receive a pilot's license was the Baroness de la Roche in 1910 after an adventurous career as an automobile racer. Three years later she was awarded the Coupe Femina for a 160-mile flight that took four hours.

The first American woman to be licensed was a Boston newspaperwoman named Harriet Quimby, in 1911. Louis Blériot had flown across the Channel in 1909, and shortly after qualifying as a pilot, Miss Quimby was determined to be the first woman to make the same flight. A slender, attractive young woman, Miss Quimby made her attempt in a Blériot monoplane. Her costume was gorgeously outlandish, a high-necked blouse and full bloomers fashioned from purple satin, with kid boots laced to her knees. The outfit was topped by goggles, gauntlets, and a long leather coat.

A purple apparition, perhaps, but she managed to fly her monoplane from Deal, England, to Epihen, France. Flying at the 6,000-foot level she ran into heavy clouds and might have strayed off course if she hadn't carried a pocket compass. A few months later, on July 1, 1912, Miss Quimby was killed when her plane crashed during a Boston air show.

The second American woman pilot was Mathilde Moisant, whose brother John operated a flying school on Long Island and managed a troupe of exhibition fliers. After her brother was killed, Mathilde took over the troupe for a brief but exciting aerial career. At an exhibition in Wichita Falls, Texas, she insisted on taking off despite a high wind. The plane crashed on takeoff, but Mathilde was hauled out of the wreckage with singed hair and leggings after the gasoline tank exploded. Her family then insisted that she stop flying and bought her a plantation in Central America as a reward for hanging up her goggles.

Probably the most famous of the prewar female pilots was Ruth Law, who held the third license granted an American woman. More than any other of her sex, until

Amelia Earhart's generation came along, she was filled with the competitive spirit. Shortly after Victor Carlstrom attempted a nonstop flight from Chicago to New York, which ended in Erie, Pennsylvania, when a fuel line broke and he was forced down, Ruth Law made a try at the same exploit. In December of 1916 she took off from Grant Park in Chicago, skimming through the Loop at a 200-foot altitude and maneuvering between the taller buildings. Her tank held only 53 gallons, but extra containers filled all the available space in her little Curtiss D.

Navigational aids were at a premium in those days, and the intrepid Miss Law had only a compass and a clock to guide her cross-country. She also carried a barograph which would testify that she had not landed anywhere along the flight.

In an open cockpit, muffled in wool and leather, she stuck it out against the biting winds and the December cold. Five and a half hours later she was forced to land at Hornell, New York—128 miles farther up the line than Carlstrom—when her gasoline supply was exhausted. She landed in a farmyard, refueled, and doggedly continued the flight to New York City. Her engine began sputtering by the time she reached the Harlem River, and she had to make a dead-stick landing on Governor's Island. Her reception at that military post was an indication of the honors and rewards waiting for the pioneers of aviation. She was greeted by General Leonard Wood and the polar explorers Amundsen and Peary and was given $2,500 and the Aero Club's Medal of Merit as the bands played and the troops paraded. For several years Miss Law barnstormed the country, but she had retired by the time Amelia was learning to fly.

Another celebrated woman flier of the years preceding World War I was Katherine Stinson, whose brothers were also aviation pioneers and plane builders. She was a tiny girl who weighed about one hundred pounds and had to stand up in her cockpit in order to be seen by the airfield crowds when she made one of her record cross-country hops.

Katherine Stinson, as Ruth Law's chief feminine rival, decided she could better Miss Law's distance record. Flying the same route, she also took off from Grant Park in Chicago. She managed to reach Binghamton, New York, and established a new record of 783 miles nonstop, broke her propeller on landing, but carried on to land at a field on Sheepshead Bay. Like other early birds, she used railroad maps to guide her across the country.

Her younger sister, Marjorie, succumbed to the family fascination with airplanes and at the age of eighteen, in 1914, presented herself at the Wright brothers' flying school in Dayton, Ohio. She looked even younger than she was, and the Wrights wouldn't consider accepting her as a student until her parents had telegraphed their consent. Five men were her classmates, and it took six weeks for her to put in enough time behind the dual controls of a training plane to solo.

Marjorie Stinson distinguished herself by acting as an unofficial instructor for the Canadian Royal Flying Corps. She was an accomplished pilot by 1917, when four Canadians sent her a telegram asking if she could teach them to fly well enough to join the air force. She could and did and subsequently trained about fifty others for the same service.

Some very intrepid young women had broken Amelia's path to the American skyways.

One Sunday in October, 1922, Amelia rather mysteriously slipped her sister and father a pair of tickets for an air show to be held at Rogers Field and indicated they might find it interesting.

Temporary bleachers had been set up for the crowd on the field. Shortly after they were seated Muriel and her father heard an announcement on the loudspeaker system: Miss Amelia Earhart was going to try for a new women's altitude record in her Kinner Canary under the auspices of the California Aero Club. A sealed barograph for measuring altitude had been placed in her plane.

She soared to 14,000 feet, a new women's record, before her engine conked out. It was a risky business, venturing almost three miles above the earth in a plane powered by a three-cylinder, sixty-horsepower engine, but she landed safely. She ignored the cheers when she landed and immediately conferred with the mechanics on the field to learn why the engine had quit on her. The spark control lever, they said, had become disconnected during a test run. To her father and sister she explained that she didn't care much about setting new records "except that it will help Bill Kinner sell his planes."

The record, in fact, stood only a few weeks before another woman pilot, Ruth Nichols, later a close friend, climbed to a still higher altitude.

Amelia's competitive sense was well developed by then. Her determination to recapture the women's altitude championship betrayed her into pushing herself and her plane so relentlessly it almost cost her her life.

She took the Kinner Canary up into a high battlement of clouds and began flying blind. A dangerous euphoria, something like that which grips deep-sea divers, seized her and kept her pulling back on the stick. As she related, "From the sight of cities and the glistening sea two miles below, I plunged into a rolling bank of clouds. There was snow inside. It stung my face and plastered my goggles."

At that point a sensible veteran pilot—if any existed in those days—would have nosed down and abandoned the attempt to set a new record. She climbed to 11,000 feet, at which level the snow turned to sleet, then into dense fog at 12,000 feet.

There were no instruments to guide her, and she had entered a sort of limbo. Later she noted that "human sensations fail when one is thus 'blind.' Deprived of a horizon, a flier may lose the feel of his position in space. Was I flying one wing high? Was I turning? I couldn't be sure. I tried to keep the plane in flying trim, with one wish growing stronger every moment—to see the friendly earth again."

Unwisely, she took a chance, pulled the stick back, and kicked the rudder to send the plane into a spin. Down, down she spiraled through the heavy overcast, letting gravity, a dangerous copilot, take over the controls.

Fortunately she managed to zoom out of the spin at 3,000 feet after the earth became visible again.

Jauntily, but shaking inside, knowing that she would have crashed if her tiny engine had failed to start and pull her out of the spin, she vaulted out of the plane. She took off her helmet and combed her short curly hair with her fingers.

"What the hell were you trying to do?" shouted

another pilot, running over to her across the adobe. "You came down like a bullet. Suppose the overcast had closed in completely? You'd have come all the way down, and we'd've had to dig you out in pieces."

"Yes," Amelia replied coolly, "I suppose you would."

CHAPTER 4

DOING GOOD IN BOSTON

LONG IN THE MAKING, NEVER CLOSE TO healing despite the best efforts by their daughters, the breach between Amy and Edwin Earhart was deemed irreparable, unbearable, by the summer of 1924. They decided to recognize the hopelessness of staying together and agreed that Edwin should obtain an uncontested divorce while Amy went East with their daughters.

Amelia was persuaded to give up flying, for the time being at least, and accompany her mother and sister to Boston. Muriel and Amelia would complete their education and get teaching jobs. She sold her much-prized Kinner Canary and bought a Kissel touring car to drive her mother and sister across the country.

Actually, Amelia was biding her time, doing her duty,

26

willing to wear skirts and study or teach to please her mother, but with her heart still in the skies, her real ambition aloft in a cockpit. The way she drifted from school to job, back and forth, during the next several years indicated that there was no deep satisfaction in a humdrum existence of educating or being educated. She dropped in at Columbia for a semester, then dropped out again. She taught English to the foreign-born under the University of Massachusetts extension program for helping them to gain U.S. citizenship. She spent the summer of 1925 as a student at the Harvard summer school. Muriel was teaching English in a junior high school and urged her to try the pleasures of instructing the young, but Amelia was too restless—perhaps aware that she could never be happy with her feet on the ground—for a teaching career.

A half-dozen years later she would boast that she had held twenty-eight different jobs in her short life and hoped to have two hundred twenty-eight more. "Experiment! Meet new people. That's better than a college education," she declared in 1932. "You will find the unexpected everywhere as you go through life. By adventuring about, you become accustomed to the unexpected. The unexpected then becomes what it really is—the inevitable."

She had to find something more exciting than teaching middle-class children in a middle-class suburb, something that would stretch her capabilities in a new direction.

Early in autumn of 1926 she decided that settlement-house work might provide the challenge she was looking for. She presented herself at Denison House on Tyler Street, a neighborhood populated mostly by Italian, Syrian, and Chinese immigrants, with a sprinkling of Irish; it was the second oldest settlement house in Boston. There was a position open for an apprentice social worker which paid $60 a month.

Among her duties at the settlement house were teaching classes in English for the foreign-born, both children in the daytime and adults at night. She also taught prekindergarten classes and both study and games for girls five to fourteen years old. In less than a year Amelia had shown herself so adept at the work of Denison House that she was promoted to full-time resident worker.

But she still heard the "sound of wings." She could never quite forget the exhilaration, the freedom and exalted loneliness of her flights over Los Angeles. She could never feel so vibrantly alive as when she entrusted her life to a wood and canvas contraption and its tiny temperamental engine. Nor was that piercing nostalgia lessened when she learned that the man who bought her Kinner Canary—her "little sandpiper," as she fondly called it—had crashed while stunting and lost his life. No doubt that interest was heightened in 1927 when young Charles A. Lindbergh made his solo flight across the Atlantic and became the most admired person in the world; perhaps even then she was wondering why there shouldn't be a female counterpart of Lindbergh.

William Kinner, from whom she had bought her first plane, wrote from Los Angeles asking her to help find someone who could establish a sales agency for his product. One of the people she met while scouting around for an agent was Harold T. Dennison, an architect with a side interest in aviation. Dennison owned a large plot of marshland and had turned it into a landing field of sorts. He also proposed to form a corporation which would build a commercial airport and persuaded Amelia to join his board of directors.

She began flying again on weekends, mainly to demonstrate the Kinner Canary for prospective buyers.

One afternoon in April, 1928, a pivotal event in Amelia's life occurred. Amelia was rehearsing a group of children for a settlement house play and one of the other Denison House workers interrupted the rehearsal to tell her that there was a telephone call. Amelia replied that she was busy and suggested that the caller be told to try again later.

She tore herself away from the rehearsal only after the caller insisted it was important that he talk to Amelia immediately.

"My name is Railey," the caller informed her. "Captain Hilton Railey."

"Yes?"

"You're interested in flying, I understand," Captain Railey said.

"I certainly am," Amelia briskly retorted.

"Miss Earhart, would you be willing to do something important for the cause of aviation?"

"Such as what?"

"Flying a plane across the Atlantic."

She paused for only a moment. "Yes," she answered. "Who could refuse a chance like that?"

In those few seconds she made herself a candidate for legendary fame.

CHAPTER 5

PROSPECTS OF GLORY

AMELIA SUSPECTED AT FIRST THAT THE CALL from Captain Railey might be a hoax or practical joke until she checked and found out that he was a respectable Southern gentleman who now headed a public relations firm with such aerial notables as Sir Hubert Wilkins, Commander Richard E. Byrd, Lincoln Ellsworth, and Ruth Nichols among his clients.

Railey was a man in his early thirties with an adventurous background. He was born in New Orleans and became a newspaperman in his native city, Philadelphia, and New York. He served in the Army as a captain during World War I.

On a business trip to New York late in April, 1928, Railey dropped in at publisher George Palmer Putnam's office. Putnam suggested that Railey investigate a report that a wealthy woman had bought Byrd's tri-motored Fokker and planned to fly the Atlantic.

What was Putnam's interest in the matter, Railey had inquired.

"Well," Putnam replied, "if it's true we'll crash the gate. Find out all you can. Locate the ship. Pump the pilots. Chances are they know all about it. Maybe there's nothing to it. But let me know what you pick up."

The "gate-crashing" suggested by Putnam was soon accomplished. Captain Railey hurried back to Boston and before midnight had tracked down the information that Byrd's Fokker was being refitted with floats at the East Boston airport. He scouted around town until he found a couple of out-of-town fliers, Wilmer Stultz and Lou Gordon, at the Copley Plaza Hotel.

Stultz was "tight and talkative," as Railey later recalled, and admitted that he was preparing for a transatlantic flight under hush-hush conditions. In an unguarded moment, however, Stultz let it slip that a man named David T. Layman was his contact with the group sponsoring the flight. With that name, Putnam and Railey were able to solve the mystery and penetrate the secrecy surrounding the projected flight. They also managed to persuade the sponsors to allow them to take over the arrangements.

•   •   •

Of all that backstage maneuvering, Amelia knew nothing the afternoon she went over to interview with Railey. She did learn that she was being seriously considered for a well-financed venture to fly the Atlantic. An essential ingredient of the plan was that a woman, preferably a flier herself, accompany the flight, though a male pilot would be at the controls.

Ocean-hopping had fevered the public imagination for the past decade. Aviation enthusiasts regarded such flights as advancing the air age, aside from their adventurous aspects. The biggest headlines of the twenties were reserved for the transocean fliers, beginning in 1919 when Lieutenant Commander Cummings Read and a five-man crew flew a U.S. Navy amphibian to the Azores and Portugal. The transpacific flight of the *Southern Cross,* a big flying boat, was another stirring achievement. The most exciting event of that decade of many first-time achievements in long-range aviation was Lindbergh's solo flight to Paris in May of 1927.

Just after the Lindbergh flight, Mrs. Frederick Guest of London decided that it was time a woman flew the Atlantic. She bought the tri-motored Fokker *Friendship* from Commander Byrd for that purpose. She had cast herself in the role of a "Lady Lindy," whose flight from the United States to England would foster goodwill between the countries of her birth and her adoption.

Her grown children talked Mrs. Guest out of risking her own neck on such a chancy proceeding, but she insisted the flight must be made. She would finance it, and "an American girl of the right image" would take her place aboard the *Friendship*.

In Boston Railey sought advice from retired Rear Admiral Reginald K. Belknap, who told him, "I know a young social worker who flies. I'm not sure how many hours she's had, but I do know she's deeply interested in aviation and a thoroughly fine person. Call Denison House and ask for Amelia Earhart."

From his first glimpse of Miss Earhart, Railey was certain he'd found the right girl; she was young (twenty-nine), competent-looking, coolheaded enough to ask for his "personal references" before he could ask for hers. Best of all, she looked enough like Charles Lindbergh to be his sister, with the same tousled blond hair, shyness, modesty, and all-American grin, and underlying them the same hard-rock sense of purpose. At first sight Railey was convinced that she was "qualified as a person, if not as a pilot."

Railey was also impressed by her poker face when he suddenly asked, "How would you like to be the first woman to fly the Atlantic?"

As he recalled, "Only a flicker in her cool eyes betrayed the excitement this question must have aroused; calmly she asked for details—whatever I was at liberty to tell her. While I was certain in my own mind that she'd prove acceptable to Mrs. Guest, whose name I withheld, I was compelled to add that of course I could advance no such guarantee. It developed that Miss Earhart had owned several planes and had flown more than five hundred hours. . . . At the time, however, she was unable to fly with the aid of instruments alone, and her experience with tri-motored ships had been inconsequential. With intense interest I observed and appraised her as she talked. Her resemblance to Colonel Lindbergh was so extraordinary that I couldn't resist the impulse to ask her to remove her hat. She complied, brushing back her naturally tousled, wind-swept hair, and her laugh was infectious. . . . Most of all I was impressed by the poise of the boyish figure at my desk. There was warmth and dignity in her manner, her speech." Amelia Earhart, he felt, was not merely the "norm" of American women but their "sublimation."

It was only later that Captain Railey reflected, in a newspaper article, on the consequences of his choice, which transformed her "from an obscure social worker, absorbed in the lives of children at a Boston settlement house, to a world figure in aviation and the honored guest of kings and queens."

He wondered why she had allowed herself to be

recruited when "even to her it must have seemed a stunt without constructive benefit to the aeronautical industry" and why afterward she went on risking her life for records and newspaper headlines. His answer was that she was driven on by internal and external pressures. "She was caught up in the hero racket that compelled her to strive for increasingly dramatic records, bigger and braver feats that automatically insured the publicity necessary to the maintenance of her position as the foremost woman pilot in the world. She was a victim of an era of 'hot' aeronautics that began with Lindbergh and Byrd and that shot 'scientific' expeditions across continents, oceans, and polar regions by dint of individual exhibition." But all those facets of the "hero racket" were invisible the day of that first interview. He shot a series of practical questions at her, rapid fire, as she recalled in *The Fun of It*:

Was I willing to fly the Atlantic?

In the event of disaster would I release those in charge from all responsibility?

What was my education—if any?

How strong was I?

How willing?

How much flying experience?

What would I do after the flight?

• • •

Railey apparently was satisfied with her answers. She told him she had five hundred hours in the air, and though there would be a male pilot and a mechanic, she hoped to take a turn at the controls. She also admitted that she had not learned to fly by instruments and that she had never handled a plane with more than one engine.

The feminist in her must have flinched slightly when Railey informed her that the pilot would be paid $20,000 and the mechanic $5,000, but her only compensation would be the privilege of making the flight. Even the fees from any newspaper stories she might write about her experience would have to be turned over to the backer.

She was then dispatched to New York for an appearance before the Putnam-Layman-Phipps screening committee. Putnam was the chief inquisitor, his qualifications being the fact that he was the publisher and a personal friend of Lindbergh and others associated with the world of adventure and exploration.

The interview, she reflected later, "found me in a curious situation. If they did not like me at all, or found me wanting in too many respects, I would be deprived of the trip. If they liked me too well, they might be loath to drown me. It was, therefore, necessary for me to maintain an attitude of impenetrable mediocrity. . . ."

Because of Mrs. Guest's insistence on secrecy, Amelia was given few details of the flight plan. She did not know when the *Friendship* would take off, who was financing the venture, who would pilot the plane. So far as the press was concerned, the tri-motored Fokker *Friendship* was still owned by Commander Byrd and being prepared for South Pole exploration. On returning to Boston and Denison House, Amelia told Marion Perkins, her supervisor, that Putnam, Layman, and Phipps had questioned her for about an hour "about my education, and work, and hobbies. I had the feeling they liked me, but, as they did not minimize the hazards of the trip, maybe that isn't good, because they may not want to put me in a situation where I may be dropped in the cold Atlantic's Davy Jones' locker. I realized that they were making me talk to see whether I dropped my 'g's' or used 'ain't,' which I'm sure would have disqualified me as effectively as failing to produce a pilot's license."

Two days later Amelia got a letter from Layman saying she had been selected for the flight and enclosing a contract embodying the terms Hilton Railey had outlined. Fame, if any, would be her only recompense. Commander Richard Byrd would be technical consultant for the flight and pick the pilot and mechanic. Technically, Amelia would be in command and make the decisions once the *Friendship* was on its way across the Atlantic.

In the next several weeks she learned a bit more about the flight and the reasons for secrecy. "Once the world knew," she later recorded (in *20 hrs. 40 min.: Our Flight in the Friendship*), "we should be submerged in a deluge of curiosity making it impossible to continue the preparations in orderly fashion. Then, too, it would do no good to aviation to invite discussion of a project some accident might delay. Actually the pontoon equipment on this type of plane was experimental, and no one could tell in advance whether or not it would prove practicable. Another objection was the possibility of instigating a 'race,' which no one wanted. . . . By our example we did not want to risk hurrying ill-prepared aspirants into the field with possibly tragic results."

Finally she was taken out to the hangar in East Boston, near the fog-shrouded waters of the harbor, for her first look at the *Friendship*. The big monoplane, German-built and a descendant of the bombers used by the Luftwaffe in World War I, was jacked up in the shadow of the hangar. "Mechanics and welders worked nearby on the struts for the pontoons that were shortly to replace the wheels. The ship's golden wings, with their spread of seventy-two feet, were strong and exquisitely fashioned. The red orange of the fuselage, though blending with the gold, was chosen not for artistry but for practical use. If we had come down orange could have been seen further than any other color."

The plan called for the *Friendship* to be flown to Trespassey Bay, Newfoundland, from which it would hop off for England. After the pontoons were fitted, it was taken on test hops over Boston Harbor to determine its load capability (it was to be equipped with two extra gas tanks holding 900 gallons) and the precision of its instruments.

Amelia finally met the two men with whom she would share the adventure. The pilot would be Wilmer Stultz, a sawed-off, blond, blue-eyed young man of German-American ancestry like Amelia. Bill Stultz was a highly skilled pilot, navigator, and radio operator, a combination of talents rarely found but absolutely essential on the *Friendship* flight. His addiction to the brandy bottle was well known, but there were few pilots of that day, Lindbergh again the exception, who weren't hard drinkers. Amelia was assured that Stultz was OK once he had his hands on the controls, but even a twenty-seven-year-old can be handicapped by a blinding hangover. He was two years younger than Amelia, had served with the 634th Aero Squadron during the war, then had joined the Navy and flown seaplanes from 1919 to 1922. Since then he had taken forty planes to Brazil for Curtiss and instructed Brazilians in how to fly them, had been a test pilot, and had bounced around as a member of the Gates Flying Circus.

Lou Gordon, the mechanic from Texas, was twenty-six years old. He was also Army-trained and had been a mechanic on the Handley Page bombers which sank two obsolete battleships off the Virginia capes in 1921 as part of General Billy Mitchell's futile campaign to convince the U.S. General Staff of the lethal worth of airpower. After being discharged from the Army in 1926, Gordon had worked for the Philadelphia Rapid Transit Air Service, serving as mechanic on Fokker tri-motors like the *Friendship* flying passengers between Philadelphia, Washington, and Norfolk.

For more than two weeks Amelia and her colleagues studied the weather reports almost hourly, waiting for a break in the pattern which made it stormy around Boston when it was clear in the mid-Atlantic, and vice versa. The waiting got on everyone's nerves, especially Stultz's. His drinking alarmed everyone, but Lou Gordon, an old friend of Stultz's and well acquainted with his reactions to the tension of waiting, assured them the pilot would be all right once they were on their way. George Putnam and

Hilton Railey did their best to distract Amelia by taking her on drives into the country and dining with her nightly.

Toward the end of May Amelia learned how tricky flying an amphibian was, how sea and weather conditions had to be just right for a takeoff. Twice in the waning days of the month Amelia, Stultz, and Gordon met at 3:30 A.M. in the lobby of the Copley Plaza, where the two men were staying, and set off for the East Boston airport with packs of sandwiches, Thermos bottles, and other gear for the flight to Newfoundland. Each time a tugboat took them out to *Friendship*. They couldn't take off either time because the fog was too thick and there wasn't enough wind to provide lift for their wings.

In a rather somber mood, Amelia wrote two short letters to her parents which were to be opened in the event that the *Friendship* didn't make it. To her father she wrote, in part, "I have no faith that we'll meet anywhere again, but I wish we might." To her mother: "Our family tends to be too secure. My life has really been very happy and I didn't mind contemplating its end in the midst of it."

On June 3 the weather reports from New York, from Britain, and from ships at sea indicated the following morning would be propitious for the first leg of the flight.

Once again the trio took off from T Wharf for the *Friend-ship*, riding on its pontoons in a gentle swell. The weather was clear, and there was a fairly brisk southeast wind.

In a few minutes, with Stultz and Gordon in the cockpit, Amelia crouched just behind them in the cabin to watch the airspeed indicator, they taxied out into the harbor. Twice Stultz gave the plane the gun and it skimmed across the waters, but the *Friendship* was unwieldy with its extra 900 gallons of gasoline. On the third try, it began to lift off. Amelia watched the airspeed indicator intently, saw the needle climb to thirty miles an hour, then forty, fifty, fifty-five, sixty . . . and they were gaining altitude. The two outboard engines sputtered from the dousing of salt water they had received.

Amelia busied herself keeping the logbook. At 7 A.M. she recorded: "Slim [Gordon] has the controls and Bill [Stultz] is tuning in. He has been getting our position. I squat on the floor next to the motion picture camera with my feet in a dunnage bag. There is one man's shoe in the passageway between the gas tanks. It looks odd, but no one cares about its out-of-placedness."

Just about then, Putnam and Railey were passing on the news to press associations and newspapers that the *Friendship* had taken off on the first leg of a flight to England with the first woman ever to fly the Atlantic.

From that moment Amelia was a celebrity and would be surrounded by its pleasures and perils until her death.

At 7:30 A.M. she wrote in the logbook: "Ninety-six miles out (1 hour). 2500 feet. Bill shows me on the map that we are near Cash's Ledge. We cannot see anything (if there is anything to see) as the haze makes the visibility poor. The sun is blinding in the cockpit and will be, for a couple of hours. Bill is crouching by the hatchway, taking sights."

At 8:45 they approached the coast of Nova Scotia, well pleased that they were averaging 114 miles an hour with the help of a tail wind. "What a jagged coast," Amelia noted in the log. "There are few roads. Many little houses nestle in the woods seemingly out of communication with anything for miles. One can see deeply into the water and mark shoals and currents. What an easy way to see what are bugaboos for surface craft. . . . The ship flies smoothly, but I know a smaller one would be tossed about. . . . Our shadow skims over the treetops. The people whom I cannot see are probably used to the sight and sound of strange planes. . . . The motors are humming sweetly."

So sweetly that they lulled her to sleep. When she awoke, they were flying into a heavy fogbank off Halifax. "Since I last wrote we have circled the harbor [of] Halifax twice and slipped to a landing. Bill went 30 miles beyond and found fog to the treetops, so came back to the clearing here. The natives are swarming to the shore and several dinghies are coming out. Bill and Slim are going over to the land and get reports with the hope we can go on later. I am to stay aboard now, as we all are, later, if there is a chance of continuing. The mournful sound of the fog horn disturbs my peace and hope. I hardly think we could take off here even without fog, as there is no wind at all. Well, anyway, I'd rather visit Halifax this way than any other I can think of. . . ."

Stultz and Gordon returned to the *Friendship* with the latest weather reports. They indicated the weather was closing in, but Stultz decided to try to make Trespassey Bay that day. Halifax was only halfway on the first leg. But they were delayed while Gordon soldered a broken primer. Stultz, knowing the fog would be even thicker along the Newfoundland coast up ahead, decided they would have to spend the night in or around Halifax. Reporters and photographers swarmed around while they tried to settle in at a hotel.

The next morning, Stultz took the *Friendship* aloft for the rest of the flight to Trespassey Bay. Looking out the window, Amelia saw a small steamer off to the starboard. "I wonder," she wrote in the logbook, "if she knows who we are. I wonder if we know."

It was a smooth flight, and "weather conditions were

so nearly ideal that had it not been necessary to refuel, we should have passed Newfoundland by entirely and continued on our way eastward." Around noon they lunched off the food which had been prepared two days before by the Copley Plaza in Boston. "The tactical error was putting all the ham sandwiches on the top layer. We never got beyond them. Later, to our chagrin, we discovered that below there were similar layers of delicious chicken and tongue sandwiches, hard boiled eggs and much beside. We never had the courage to determine exactly what else there might have been."

Shortly after she reflected that the "sea looks like the back of an elephant," the coast of Newfoundland came into view. Just after 3 P.M. they glided down onto the waters off Trespassey. Almost immediately, they were surrounded by a flotilla of small boats and an almost hysterical unofficial welcoming committee of Newfoundlanders. It looked like a maritime rodeo, with the boatmen hurling ropes at the *Friendship,* Gordon out on a pontoon trying to ward them off, and Stultz cursing fervently because the ropes might foul his propellers.

They finally managed to get ashore, just before a howling gale swept in from the sea. The next day Gordon busied himself with repairs to the Fokker, and Stultz, who could not abide the tension of waiting, fretted and paced. Amelia explored the little fishing village with its frame houses and whitewashed fences. "I could enjoy myself were it not for the anxiety about a takeoff . . . and the disgusting news of publicity. Every few minutes a telegraph operator patters over and hands me a telegram from someone. Some are lovely, and others disturb me greatly. The latest says Boston papers carry a story I went to recoup fallen fortunes of family." Back in Boston her mother and sister learned the news that Amelia would fly the Atlantic from the newspapers: GIRL PILOT DARES THE ATLANTIC. Before they could get over the shock they were surrounded by reporters and photographers. Mrs. Earhart grimly refused to be interviewed, stating firmly that "in my day nice people had their names in the paper only when they were born, married, and died."

She received a telegram from Amelia in Trespassey: KNOW YOU WILL UNDERSTAND WHY I COULD NOT TELL PLANS OF FLIGHT. DON'T WORRY. NO MATTER WHAT HAPPENS IT WILL HAVE BEEN WORTH THE TRYING. LOVE, AMELIA.

Amelia and her companions stayed with a family in one of the larger houses at Trespassey. They had hoped to be able to take off for England in two or three days, but the weather was against them. "The wind held the key to our problems," as Amelia explained in *20 Hrs. 40 Min.* "For three days it blew briskly from the northwest. This was ideal for the flight itself, but far from ideal locally, as it stirred up such a sea it was impossible to load the gasoline with safety. What's more, Bill feared that the heavy weight of the load left on board the *Friendship* might seriously injure it as it was buffeted about in the rough water."

They were stalled, as it turned out, for thirteen nerve-grating days.

Amelia, always strong-nerved, busied herself with walking along the beaches, reading (*The Story of the Titanic,* one of the few books available, the great liner having struck an iceberg and sunk off the Newfoundland coast), and playing cards with Gordon. The tall, handsome Texan was equally calm about the delays. The problem was the high-strung Bill Stultz, who again resorted to the brandy bottle. On June 7 she wrote in her log, "The men are simply great under the strain"—but that was only for the record. Stultz, in fact, was close to cracking up—a possibility the flight's backers had foreseen by keeping a standby pilot, Lou Gower, waiting in Boston to take his place if necessary.

Amelia decided to take a big-sisterly tack: She was two years older and stood two or three inches above the runtish Stultz. Several times she persuaded him to go fishing, eeling, or hiking along the rocky coast with her and leave the bottle behind. Each time, Stultz either produced a bottle hidden on his person and had to be led back to Trespassey or would suddenly start walking back to the village.

A dozen days went by, with the tension becoming almost unbearable, yet in her official account Amelia would tactfully assert that her most outstanding memories of Trespassey were "the lovely hooked rugs and the excellent trout streams of Newfoundland."

On the evening of June 16 Amelia and Lou Gordon were playing rummy in the front parlor of the house where they were staying. Overhead they could hear Stultz staggering around his room. Would he ever sober up, they wondered, or was it time to telegraph the backers to have Lou Gower sent up to replace him? They agreed that Stultz was the better pilot of the two, and maybe they'd wait another day before deciding what to do.

They were playing a last round when the doorbell jangled. A messenger from the telegraph office was at the door. He brought a message from New York saying the New York weather forecaster, whose reports they had chiefly been relying on, finally announced that he could promise fair weather over the Grand Banks and the North Atlantic for the next forty-eight hours.

"What about Bill?" Amelia asked Gordon. "Will he be able to fly?"

"Once he gets in the cockpit and instinct takes over. . . ."

Amelia slept fitfully that night, was the first up in the morning, and woke up her two companions.

Gordon got Stultz on his feet somehow, applied cold water outside and hot coffee inside. Even so, Amelia and Gordon almost had to carry the little man down the steep rocky path from the house to the waterfront. They stuffed him into the *Friendship*'s cockpit; he stared blearily at the sunlit waters of the harbor, and they could only hope for the best.

Gordon kept reassuring Amelia that Stultz would be all right once they were under way, but Amelia kept thinking of all those hours of flying ahead. And not only the actual flying but doing the navigating and operating the radio. The prospects seemed even dimmer when she searched around the back of the plane and found that Stultz had stashed a brandy bottle, though Gordon claimed that Stultz never took a swig when he was at the controls. Amelia decided not to take a chance and dumped the bottle over the side.

Now the problem was taking off, getting up the necessary speed on pontoons to lift three tons into the air. They had already jettisoned all the excess baggage and reduced the extra gasoline carried in the two tanks behind the cockpit from 900 to 700 gallons, a fuel margin so slender that Stultz thought they might have to come down along the Irish coast. The only food they brought was scrambled-egg sandwiches, coffee, a few oranges, chocolate, and a bottle of malted milk tablets, plus five gallons of water. They had no clothing except that which they wore.

Three times Stultz taxied over the harbor waters at maximum speed, struggling to get the Fokker into the sky; the plane vibrated under the effort until it seemed all the fittings would be shaken loose. On the fourth pass the *Friendship* finally lurched off the choppy surface of Trespassey Bay, the engines sputtered from their intake of salt water but achieved a steady roar at last, and the airspeed dial pointed to 60 mph. They gained altitude, shook themselves free of land and sea, and headed for the horizon.

CHAPTER 6

LANDFALL

WHEN THE *FRIENDSHIP* FINALLY MADE IT into the skies off Newfoundland, Amelia was already concentrating on the job at hand: the logbook. A man's jottings would have been matter-of-fact, but Amelia saw things with the eye of a thwarted poet.

She noted airspeeds, altitudes, sky and sea conditions, but she also scribbled down what would have seemed to a veteran airman her feminine impressions. Off Cape Race the view below was fleeced with fog, and she wrote in the log, "I know (the Irish writer, Lord) Dunsany would like to see the world above the earth. Irish fogs have been described in detail, and their bilious effect, and their fairies and their little people. But no one has written of a bird's-eye view of one from an imaginative eye."

They had taken off shortly after 11 A.M. on June 17, and by noon Bill Stultz's eyes had cleared and his hands were steady on the controls. He performed all his three-in-one functions efficiently. It was almost incredible how he pulled himself together once he was free of the earth. Amelia could only congratulate herself (and Gordon) on sticking with him.

Soon they ran into a line storm and bucked strong head winds and pelting rain. Then the horizon cleared, and Amelia was able to confide to the log, "140 m.p.h. now. Wonderful time. Temp. 52. The heater from cockpit warms the cabin too. . . . Bill says radio is cuckoo. He is calling now. . . . I have just uncurled from lying on Major Woolley's suit for half an hour. . . . There is nothing to see but churned mist, very white in the afternoon sun. . . ."

She crouched at the chart table and spent most of her time staring out the small square window nearby. The role of passenger was discomfiting, and she may already have been thinking of making this flight solo. When she wasn't observing and taking notes, she slipped into the cockpit behind the two men and watched how they coaxed the best possible performance out of the *Friendship*. If Amelia ever flew the Atlantic alone, she would have to acquire the combined skills of Bill Stultz and Lou Gordon, and they were the best in the business.

At 4:15 P.M. they were still riding out the drifts of fog and cloud with the sea barely visible. Stultz began climbing above the 4,000-foot altitude to surmount the overcast. By radio he contacted a British ship below and got their bearings. "I do believe we are getting out of the fog," she observed. "Marvellous shapes in white stand out, some trail shimmering veils. The clouds look like icebergs in the distance. It seemed almost impossible to believe that one couldn't bounce forever on the packed fog we are leaving. The highest peaks of the fog mountains . . . are tinted pink, with the setting sun. The hollows are grey and shadowy. . . . We are 1096 miles out. . . . The view is too vast and lovely for words. I think I am happy—sad admission of scant intellectual equipment."

Soon nightfall blotted out the view, and Amelia dined off a handful of malted-milk tablets. There was little talk among the three; all were intent on their jobs. The only light came from the illuminated radium dials on the instrument panel. The only sound was of the steady drumming of the engines. So far it had been a marvelously smooth flight, with all the equipment functioning perfectly.

" . . . A night of stars. North the horizon is clear cut. To the south it is a smudge. The exhausts send out glowing meteors. How marvelous is a machine and the mind that made it. "Bill sits up alone. Every nerve and muscle alert. Many hours to go. "

For hours they had been flying by instruments, rising to the 11,000-foot level, with nothing on which they could take a bearing. Unvoiced but nagging, there was the fear that they might be far off course, lost in an endless blur of fog and cloud. It got so cold in the cabin that Amelia gratefully climbed into the fur-lined flying suit lent her by Major Woolley of Boston. They had been in the air for more than sixteen hours and had a fuel supply for only four or five hours left. If Stultz's navigation was on the mark, they should soon be approaching the Irish and English coasts. If not . . . but no one spoke of that.

As dawn flushed the skies ahead of them, they began descending, venturing back into the fog and mist. "Going down fast. It takes a lot to make my ears hurt. 5000 [feet] now. Awfully wet. Water dripping in window. Port motor coughing. Sounds as if all motors were cutting. Bill opens her wide to try to clear her. Sounds rotten on the right. . . . Fog awful. Motors better, but not so good. . . . We are going to go into, under or over a storm. I don't like to, with one motor acting the way it does. . . ."

Finally, with great relief, they rode out the murk and turbulence, and at the 3,000-foot level they caught sight of the sea below. Amelia's jubilation was evident in her jottings: "The sea! We are 3000. Patchy clouds. We have been jazzing from 1000 to 5000 where we now are, to get out of the clouds. At present there are sights of blue and sunshine, but everlasting clouds are always in the offing. The radio is dead."

But they still didn't know where they were. Relying on dead reckoning, they decided that they should be catching a glimpse of the Irish coast any minute now, but there was nothing but sea ahead and below. The fuel supply would allow them not much more than an hour in the air. " 'Mess,' " she later wrote, "epitomized the blackness of the moment. Were we beaten? We all favored sticking to the course. We had to. With faith lost in that, it was hopeless to carry on. Besides, when last we checked it, before the radio went dead, the plane had been holding true."

Suddenly they sighted a big luxury liner furrowing the seas below—the *America*. They circled the ship, tried frantically to get the radio operating again so they could receive their exact position.

Finally, in desperation, Amelia wrapped a note around an orange, tied it with silver string, and placed it in a paper bag. An amateur bombardier for the moment, she dropped the message through the hatch, watched it zoom away in the slipstream. There was a hurried conference on the possibility of making a forced landing near the *America,* but Stultz judged the seas were too rough. They circled the ship again and returned to their original course.

Down below, on the bridge of the *America,* Captain Friend and his first officer had watched the approach of the *Friendship* through their binoculars.

"What's that aircraft?" Captain Friend asked. "Why's she flying so low?"

"Looks like a reconnaissance plane," his first officer speculated.

"It can't be one of ours," the captain remarked, "so it must be the Royal Navy's. They're certainly taking a lot of interest in us."

"My God," the first officer exclaimed, pointing to the brown object dropped by the *Friendship* which plummeted into the water off the *America*'s bow, "we're being bombarded!"

Still unaware that they had been buzzed by a plane from the American shore, they watched the *Friendship* continue on its way eastward.

One hour's fuel supply left, Gordon announced after making a check of the gauges. The mechanic, probably trying to reassure Amelia, came back to her post in the cabin and nonchalantly chewed on a sandwich.

Down below they sighted several small fishing boats, which indicated land could not be far away.

They strained their eyes, quartering the misty horizon for a glimpse of the land mass that must be ahead.

The ceiling had lowered to 500 feet, and they were almost skimming the rough seas below.

Suddenly a blue shadow loomed through the mist—land or another cloud bank.

It was Gordon who shouted first: "Land!"

In a moment the coastline assumed definition. They still didn't know whether they were approaching Ireland or England but agreed it looked like what they imagined an English coast would be. None of them, incidentally, had ever been farther east than Boston before.

The *Friendship* skirted the cliffs while its occupants studied the roadways, pastures, and hedgerows below. They could not venture far inland because they had only a few gallons of gasoline left in the tanks and, being equipped with pontoons, could land only on water.

When a small coastal town came into view, Stultz decided to set the plane down. The fuel supply was so low that the engines were kept going only by keeping the plane level in flight. Stultz made a perfect landing out in the Channel and taxied up to a large buoy. Gordon leaped out on a pontoon and tied up to the buoy to keep the swift-running tide from carrying the *Friendship* farther out in the Channel. "Then, having crossed the Atlantic by air, we waited for the village to come out and welcome us."

And a cool Celtic welcome it was. Three men working on a railway line on the shore closest to them hardly looked up from their labors. It was almost half an hour before a police launch came out, and the local cop demanded to know who they were and what they were doing in the harbor. He did inform them that, in just twenty hours and forty minutes, they had flown from Trespassey Bay, Newfoundland, to Burry Port, Wales, a few miles east of Swansea, and agreed to send out a boat which would haul them to a mooring for the night. But it was more than two hours before the citizens ashore bestirred themselves and towed the *Friendship* to her overnight mooring, and Amelia and her companions jumped gratefully ashore.

CHAPTER 7

INSTANT CELEBRITY

IT WAS SLOW IN GATHERING FORCE, BUT once the word got around the little Welsh port that they were transatlantic fliers a roaring welcome was organized ashore. Hilton Railey had chartered an old Imperial Airways flying boat and flown up to Burry Port.

"Congratulations!" Railey shouted. "How does it feel to be the first woman to fly the Atlantic?"

"Hello," was all she had to say for herself.

Railey noted that they were all dead weary but that there was something in her attitude besides the inevitable letdown.

"What's the matter?" he asked, sitting next to her in the doorway. "Aren't you excited?"

"Excited?" she said listlessly. "No. It was a grand experience, but all I did was lie on my tummy and take pictures of the clouds. We didn't see much of the ocean. Bill did all the flying—had to. I was just baggage, like a sack of potatoes."

"What of it? You're still the first woman to fly the Atlantic and what's more the first woman pilot."

"Oh, well," she replied with a philosophical smile, "maybe someday I'll try it alone."

The official welcome, with a committee headed by Mrs. Frederick Guest awaited them in Southampton.

They were then taken on a Rolls-Royce tour of the port, with the sidewalks lined by applauding Britons. Amelia was handed a cable of congratulations from President Coolidge which seemed to her to imply that the flight was her personal achievement. But she was too honest and forthright to let an undeserved compliment stand without being corrected, particularly since the credit belonged to a man who had surmounted personal and technical problems of almost frightful proportions. In her cabled reply she crisply informed the President:

SUCCESS ENTIRELY DUE GREAT SKILL OF MR. STULTZ STOP HE WAS ONLY ONE MILE OFF COURSE AT VALENTIA AFTER FLYING BLIND FOR TWO THOUSAND TWO HUNDRED FORTY-SIX MILES AT AVERAGE SPEED ONE HUNDRED AND THIRTEEN M.P.H.

Still wearing her flying suit, Amelia, with her flight companions, was borne off to London in a yellow Rolls.

From then on she was the center of a whirl of congratulation and adulation.

Only once did Amelia manage to play hooky from the social and official engagements made for her by the flight's backers. The person she was most eager to meet in England was Lady Heath, a sportswoman who had flown solo from Capetown to London. She finally achieved that meeting and in addition obtained Lady Heath's promise to give her the use of her plane for a few hours' recreation away from the crowds and the banquet tables.

At 5:30 one morning she slipped out of Mrs. Guest's house in Park Lane without telling anyone where she was going. She found a taxi and was driven out to the Croydon airdrome, where Lady Heath kept her Avian Moth. For two hours, alone at the controls, she flew through the morning skies, happy to be in her proper element. She was so delighted by the way the Moth handled that she made arrangements to buy the plane from Lady Heath before returning to the States.

There were a few more days of being lionized, a lunch given by American correspondents, attendance at a tattoo (a military entertainment) with pageantry supplied by the British air and ground forces, and then she and her co-heroes sailed for the United States aboard the liner *Roosevelt*.

To Captain Railey, who accompanied them on the *Roosevelt*, she confided that the only way she could live with herself in the future would be to fly the Atlantic alone. "I'm a false heroine," she explained, "and that makes me feel guilty. Someday I will redeem my self-respect. I can't live without it."

America was still crazy over transatlantic fliers and reserved her most tumultuous welcomes for them, starting with the ritual perfected by New York City, silk-hatted Mayor Jimmy Walker greeting the trio with wisecracks and a key to the city, immersion in confetti coming up Broadway in an open car. Out of the thirty-two cities which demanded the honor of receiving them, Amelia and her companions chose New York, Boston, and Chicago. In Chicago Bill Stultz disappeared, and George Putnam, not unwillingly, put on goggles and a leather jacket and took Stultz's place beside Amelia.

Putnam, in fact, was slowly taking over her life by making himself indispensable. Unofficially he acted as her manager and advised her on endorsing commercial products, lecture offers, film contracts (all rejected), pleas for articles from newspapers and magazines. Within a few months after returning to America, she had received $50,000 from various sources, mostly advertisers, and had made herself financially independent.

The aggressive Putnam, having become Amelia's closest adviser, naturally became her publisher. She went into seclusion at Putnam's home in suburban Rye, New York, to write the book about the *Friendship* flight, *20 Hrs. 40 Min.,* in a matter of weeks.

After finishing the book and reading the proofs, she felt an intense desire to "get away from it all," reassert herself as an individual, free herself from public demands, and think about her future. She had already decided against returning to Denison House because somehow fame and social work didn't go together: "For the moment," she said, "all I wished to do in the world was to be a vagabond—in the air."

The swift, maneuverable little Avian she had bought from Lady Heath in England had arrived, and she decided to take off alone on a series of hops across the country to the Pacific Coast. Incidentally, it would be the first time a woman had ever flown from the Atlantic to the Pacific and back again. In 1928 flying across the country was still difficult. One small town looked pretty much like another, there were few airports, and the transcontinental pilot had to rely on landmarks, railways, rivers, and other features of the terrain.

Nor were the airports all they should have been. Landing at Rogers Field near Pittsburgh, the airstrip was grass-covered. She made a neat three-point landing but then the Avian struck a shallow ditch concealed by grass and almost flipped over. The propeller was cracked, and Amelia had to lay over in Pittsburgh while spare parts were flown out from New York.

She made Fort Worth safely in a series of flights, but negotiating Texas, with its vast plains and empty horizons, was almost like flying the Atlantic. Soon after leaving Fort Worth she was thrown off course when she and the Avian were shaken up and bounced around by air pockets. Worse yet, her map, which had been fastened to her shirt with a safety pin, had been blown out of the cockpit.

She kept on flying what she hoped was the right course westward until she came to a highway, which she followed into New Mexico. Her gas supply was getting low, and the sun was setting. There were plenty of automobiles on the highway below but only an occasional lonely ranch house or oil derrick to indicate the country had been settled. It was getting dark and her tanks were almost empty when she sighted a small town ahead; Hobbs, New Mexico, as she was to learn shortly. The only feasible landing place was the main street, which fortunately was empty of traffic at the dinner hour. "At high altitude where the air is thin," she later recounted, "it is necessary to make a pretty fast landing, so I am afraid I broke speed ordinances as the Avian rolled smartly through the heart of the city." Hobbs was an oil boom town just six months old when Amelia Earhart dropped out of the sky. "The citizens helped me fold the wings and then, after sending telegrams by way of the single telephone, I dined at the Owl Cafe, from the much appreciated but invariable menu of fried eggs, coffee and bread. And the luxury of a real bed!"

Amelia was way off her intended course and next morning started back for Texas and her scheduled destination, El Paso. Once again she got lost and this time came down at Pecos, Texas, with one of the tires on her landing wheels flat from a thorn puncture. The natives not only repaired her tire but carried her off to a Rotary luncheon. Taking off for El Paso that afternoon, the Avian developed engine trouble, and Amelia had to make a forced landing in the mesquite. Once again luck was with her. She had come down near a highway, and a number of motorists soon sped to her assistance. The plane was towed back to Pecos and a three-day layover waiting for spare parts to arrive from El Paso.

She made it to Los Angeles in time to watch the start of

the National Air Races, then flew back East with only a few minor mishaps to mar the journey.

On her return to New York early in the autumn of 1928, Amelia found that George Putnam, as her agent, had lined up more lecture engagements than she could have fulfilled. She had received an offer from *Cosmopolitan* magazine to join their staff. For the next year Amelia turned out an article almost every month for *Cosmopolitan* on subjects that interested her, all of them dealing with aviation.

Eventually, perhaps inevitably, Amelia found the work too confining. Also, in the back of her mind there was the idea of vindicating herself for the "false" fame, as she regarded it, which she had acquired on the *Friendship* flight. For the next several years much of her life was filled with preparations aimed in the general direction of eventually flying the Atlantic by herself.

Early in 1929 it was announced that the first Women's Air Derby—journalistically retitled the "powder puff derby"—would be held that August. Amelia promptly sold her lightweight Avian and bought a Lockheed Vega, which was more powerful, a high-wing monoplane capable of longer and faster flights. From now on, her life would be devoted more to flying than to lecturing, editing, writing, or posing for photographers.

CHAPTER 8

ANGELS, SKYLARKS, AND BIRDWOMEN

ON A SUNDAY AFTERNOON, AUGUST 18, 1929, twenty planes piloted by women lined up in two rows on the runway of Clover Field near Santa Monica, California, for the first Women's Air Derby. It was regarded as the first serious test of feminine flying capabilities under the stress of competition. All twenty of the contestants, including Amelia in her Lockheed Vega, saw the cross-country race as a critical challenge. Under the headline WOMEN'S DERBY SHOULD BE TERMINATED, one of the Los Angeles newspapers stated that challenge: "Women have been dependent on men for guidance for so long that when they are put on their own resources they are handicapped."

The contestants were outraged by that and other slurs; they saw the race (as Louise Thaden said) as "more important than life or death." Editorial gibes were answered by the Race Committee: "We wish officially to thumb our noses at the press."

Thirteen of the planes were entered in the heavier and more powerful-engined class, including Amelia's, and the others competed in the light-plane class.

One by one, at one-minute intervals, the score of contestants took off at a wave of the starter's flag. The race to Cleveland was to take eight days, with prearranged stops each day and no night flying permitted. The first overnight stop was at San Bernardino, California, which all but one of the entrants made.

Amelia herself almost became a dropout the next day while crossing the desert to Yuma, Arizona. On landing at Yuma she ran into a sandbank and damaged her propeller. The other contestants sportingly voted to extend the layover in Yuma to three hours while the damage to Amelia's plane was repaired.

At some of the stops there were banquets; at others they were lucky to find restrooms in working order. The male speakers at some of the festivities along the way insisted on referring to the contestants as angels or ladybirds and the race itself as a lipstick or powder puff or petticoat derby. Amelia would smile bravely or grimly at such remarks, then advise the male banqueters that they were to be called fliers or pilots, that they had earned the right to equal dignity with male aviators.

There were accidents along the way—one of them fatal. Marvel Crosson, as her rivals learned in Fort Worth, had crashed in the Gila River country south of Phoenix. Her body was found near the wreckage with her parachute unopened. "More good pilots," the surviving contestants reassured each other, "have been killed in automobiles than will ever be killed by airplanes." Florence (Pancho) Barnes stripped off her landing gear and clipped the top off a car parked too close to the airstrip at Pecos, Texas. Blanche Noyes also suffered a mishap when her plane ground-looped on landing, but neither she nor Pancho Barnes was injured.

On the seventh day the surviving contestants reached Columbus, Ohio. Amelia and Ruth Nichols were leading the field in elapsed time, and their rivalry would be decided by who made the best time on the last hop into Cleveland. Next morning they lined up on the runway for the starter's signal. Taking off just ahead of Amelia, Miss Nichols' plane suddenly dipped its wing and crashed into a tractor parked at the end of the runway. The plane flipped over.

Instead of taking off in her turn and probably gaining an undisputed lead over the other contestants, Amelia immediately climbed out of the cockpit of her Lockheed and ran over to the wreckage of Miss Nichols' plane to haul her rival out. Miss Nichols was unhurt. Amelia then took off for Cleveland and the finish line but by then had lost her edge over the others. She finished in third place, behind Louise Thaden and Gladys O'Donnell.

Amelia was kept occupied that fall on the lecture circuit, spreading the gospel of the air age. One appearance was scheduled for Atchison, where she dedicated the new high school stadium named for her.

In aviation her overriding concern now was the development of the first passenger airlines making scheduled flights. She joined Transcontinental Air Transport, the corporate parent of Trans World Airlines, as an adviser more or less in charge of persuading women it was safe to board an airliner. Some pioneering market analysts discovered that the public's reluctance to use air transport evidently was grounded on feminine prejudice against the untried. More men would have been willing to cut their travel time, especially business executives, but were prevented from flying by their wives' fears.

Amelia not only flew a number of TAT's routes but

took charge of the traffic department and tried to iron out its difficulties with maintaining flight schedules.

She was determined that in the near future American travelers would accept airlines as a necessity rather than an exotic adventure. "Airplanes," she noted, "sometimes offered no advantages over ground facilities in time saving, if they didn't fly often enough to be a convenience to passengers."

Busy as she was with executive responsibilities, Amelia found time to widen her experience as a pilot. She set new speed records for women over 1-mile and 100-kilometer courses and began flying an autogiro, the early model of the helicopter, in which she set an altitude record of 18,415 feet.

All that was merely on the fringes of her main ambition to fly the Atlantic solo. To emulate Lindbergh and become the first woman to make that flight she needed all the piloting experience she could get, particularly over long distances, plus navigational instruction, plus some knowledge of meteorology. For the last, she went to Dr. James H. Kimball, chief meteorologist of the New York Weather Bureau, and unofficially became his pupil. She spent hours standing beside his desk in the Weather Bureau on top of the Whitehall Building in lower Manhattan, watching while he read telegraphs containing reports from land stations and ships at sea, then drew weather maps with wavy lines representing isobars, isotherms, high and low pressure areas. From Dr. Kimball, a courtly, middle-aged Southerner, she learned that storm systems generally move from west to east over the United States, that the prevailing winds over the Atlantic are westerly. She also learned that storm centers revolve in a counterclockwise fashion when north of the equator. All this was exceedingly valuable to a young woman whose aerial ambitions ranged the world. Dr. Kimball was an endlessly patient instructor because he believed that flights such as hers pioneered a regular transocean air service. This was being held up, in his opinion, only because there wasn't enough accurate weather information available.

Two years after the *Friendship* flight, three years after his own, Colonel Lindbergh was still the model, the prototype, whom Amelia looked up to with something close to hero worship.

She had become friendly with Lindbergh and his wife, the former Anne Morrow, when TAT inaugurated its coast-to-coast passenger service (forty-eight hours with frequent stopovers). Lindbergh piloted one of the inaugural flights to Los Angeles, on which Amelia and Mrs. Lindbergh were passengers. The latter had learned to fly, and Amelia admired her almost as much as her husband. "With her diminutive figure engulfed in ungainly [flying] togs, she looks like a tiny teddy bear beside her six-foot-something husband," Amelia observed.

Amelia considered the Lindberghs' an ideal marriage, not only because of its romantic aspects, but because they were both fliers. On a flight to the Orient Mrs. Lindbergh had acted as her husband's navigator and radio operator. It seemed to her that the couple shared more of their lives with each other than any other she had known.

About her own matrimonial prospects she was much more dubious. Obviously her husband could be no ordinary fellow. "Marriage is a mutual responsibility," she insisted. "And I cannot see why husbands shouldn't share in the responsibility of the home." By that, she added, she meant "something more detailed" than merely "keep a roof over the collective head and coal in the furnace." A willing and persistent suitor, though unfortunately still married, had been waiting to make Amelia his bride, even under such feminist conditions, ever since the *Friendship* flight.

CHAPTER 9

THE BRIDE WORE BROWN

THE MAN WHO MARRIES A CELEBRITY AND intends to be a husband as well as a luggage-bearing consort requires a resilient ego and a large amount of self-confidence. It helps considerably if he is successful in his own right. Even more if he is a man of affairs able and willing to spare the time to manage his wife's career.

George Palmer Putnam figured that he fulfilled the requirements. He was a hard-driving, ambitious fellow with the habit of command. He was a man of action who possessed a strongly competitive urge and he hated to lose out in anything, whether it was a business deal or a woman.

By his own account he had proposed to Amelia six times between 1928 and late 1930 and had been turned down. Amelia was wary of marriage, having been disillusioned as a child by her parents' unhappiness; furthermore, she was a feminist—as well as utterly feminine in most ways—and except for the Lindberghs', saw few happy marriages around her. She was the sort who, using up her energies in many ways, could be perfectly happy unmarried. Furthermore, her career did not lend itself to any of the ordinary restrictions and conventionalities of marriage. She was, in fact, doing beautifully on her own.

Shortly after being divorced from his third wife, Putnam proposed to Amelia in a hangar at the Lockheed aircraft factory in Burbank, California, while she was waiting for her plane to be warmed up. She listened gravely, then, to Putnam's surprise, nodded in agreement, patted him on the arm, and ran off to climb into the cockpit of her plane. Just like that. Putnam was stunned. He could hardly believe she had accepted. He did not see her until several days later, upon which she confirmed the acceptance.

Amelia rightly believed that Putnam was mature enough, self-confident enough, and generous-spirited enough to give her the freedom she required. Yet there was a last-moment wavering the morning they were married in his mother's old house in Noank, Connecticut, on February 7, 1931.

She had appeared for the ceremony, which was to be performed by a judge who was an old friend of the Putnam family, in a bridal costume only Amelia Earhart would have considered appropriate. It consisted of a brown suit, not at all new, with a crepe blouse and brown lizardskin shoes. She was hatless, as usual.

And just before the ceremony was to take place the bride-to-be handed the prospective bridegroom a letter which might—with a less stouthearted groom—have canceled the event forthwith. It was her declaration of independence, addressed to "GP" and signed "AE," and read:

There are some things which should be writ before we are married. Things we have talked over before—most of them.

You must know again my reluctance to marry, my feeling that I shatter thereby chances in work which means so much to me. I feel the move just now as foolish as anything I could do. I know there may be compensations, but have no heart to look ahead.

In our life together I shall not hold you to any medieval code of faithfulness to me, nor shall I consider myself bound to you similarly. If we can be honest I think the differences which arise may best be avoided.

Please let us not interfere with each other's work or play, nor let the world see private joys or disagreements. In this connection I may have to keep some place where I can go to be myself now and then, for I cannot guarantee to endure at all times the confinements of even an attractive cage.

I must exact a cruel promise, and this is that you will let me go in a year if we find no happiness together.

I will try to do my best in every way.

With all his self-assurance and his insight into her character, Putnam must have been chilled by that virtual ultimatum, but he smiled bravely and nodded in agreement, and the marriage took place.

Far from interfering with Amelia's career, Putnam promoted it with even greater vigor than before. Putnam kept his new wife so busy that they had no time for a honeymoon.

With his managerial flair and promotional genius, Putnam capitalized extensively on Amelia's fame. He literally made her not only a household word but a brand name. Her picture appeared on billboards advertising cigarettes (though, she admitted, she rarely smoked more than three a year herself). Amelia Earhart lightweight airplane luggage was an immediate success, with Amelia drawing royalties on every item sold. Her name appeared on the labels of a line of women's clothes, severely tailored suits, floppy pajamas, and coats with buttons shaped like bolts.

Aside from occasional disputes over the management of her career, according to those who knew them best, the Earhart-Putnam alliance worked smoothly. Amelia decided to take up her option on the marriage after the year's trial she had insisted upon, and that was the best evidence the marriage was working. She would not be dominated even by a man accustomed to dominating others. Both being businesslike people, they divided household expenses equally and placed surplus earnings in a joint savings account. Amelia believed that the strains of marriage were eased only when the wife could pay her own way. "The individual independence of dollars and cents tends to keep a healthy balance of power in the kingdom of the home. . . . Assistants more skilled than myself can be employed to substitute in the housewife role without robbing a marriage of its essence. . . . Thus—for me—can joyful luxuries like low-wing monoplanes be had—as adding to the sum total of contentment."

Putnam was even capable of laughing easily, though with a glint in his eye, when someone playfully or inadvertently addressed him as "Mr. Earhart."

CHAPTER 10

HARBOUR GRACE TO LONDONDERRY

FOR FOUR YEARS AMELIA HAD BEEN INWARDLY tormented, feeling that there was something fraudulent about her fame. She could not help wincing whenever anyone referred to her as "Lady Lindy." The title of premier woman flier of the world, she felt, had not been fairly won. It was more the product of publicity and promotion than her own accomplishments. Her career was a see-through tissue of newspaper headlines, she herself a creature of the fame-making machinery of communications.

All that time, however, she had been training herself for vindication, even if that were needed only to still her own conscience. She had logged over a thousand hours in the air. Many of those hours had been taken up by instrument flying, learning to navigate "blind" through the worst possible weather conditions. She had prepared herself in every possible way for the grueling effort of flying the Atlantic solo.

And she wanted to be the first woman to do so, even though Ruth Nichols, as usual, was breathing down her neck. Miss Nichols, in fact, had started on such a venture only the year before, but her plane had cracked up on landing at St. John, New Brunswick. She had just recovered from her injuries and was getting ready to try again.

Early in the spring of 1932, Amelia and Putnam were living at his Rye house. They invited Bernt Balchen over for lunch. The Norwegian-born Balchen had long ago proved himself over polar skies, North and South; he had participated in Amundsen's dirigible flight over the North Pole in 1926, the Richard Byrd-Floyd Bennett flight over the North Pole, the Byrd expedition to the South Pole, and other far-ranging aerial adventures.

They went out on the croquet pitch behind the garden and took up the mallets under the April sunshine. The crocuses were beginning to bloom. The oaks and elms were starting to leaf. It was a beautiful early spring day.

When they reached the middle wicket, it was obvious that Amelia's mind was focused on neither the beauty of an early spring nor the game of croquet.

She laid her mallet down suddenly, impulsively, and

announced that she wanted to tell Balchen something. Putnam knew what was coming; they had discussed it over the breakfast table one winter morning several months before.

She wanted to fly the Atlantic, she announced when they had seated themselves on a rocky ledge nearby. And she fired three questions at Balchen: "Am I ready to do it? Is the plane ready? Will you help me?"

Balchen was a deliberate man who knew that danger of any kind must be studied carefully. He also knew that Amelia had thought out the hazards of the proposed flight long before taking it up for discussion. The most important thing was whether *she* believed she could do it.

Balchen finally cleared his throat and said, "Yes, you can do it. The plane—when we are through with it—will be okay. And, yes, I will help."

It was agreed, in that informal conference under the April sun, that Balchen would act as technical adviser for the flight. He would supervise adjustments to her Lockheed Vega monoplane with the Wright Whirlwind engine. He would also serve as "cover" for the flight. Amelia insisted that all the preparations and the takeoff itself, as in the *Friendship* flight, must be kept secret. Balchen and Lincoln Ellsworth were preparing for a flight to the South Pole, and as far as the world was concerned, his work on Amelia's plane could be taken as preparations for the polar expedition.

From that April day on, preparations went forward at full tilt, with Teterboro Airport in New Jersey as their headquarters. In a hangar there Balchen and his crew of mechanics straightened out the fuselage of the Lockheed, which had been battered in various forced landings. The new supercharged 500-horsepower Wasp engine from Pratt & Whitney was installed and subjected to rigorous tests. To increase the fuel capacity extra tanks were fitted into the wings and another in the cabin, which gave the plane a cruising radius of 3,200 miles.

And there was, in those secret preparations for Amelia's solo across the Atlantic, a coincidental human link with the Apollo flights of almost four decades later. The man in charge of determining the right fuel mix at Teterboro for the hop to Newfoundland, then the jump across the Atlantic, was an Army pilot named Major Edwin Aldrin. His son would become an astronaut, a member of the Apollo crew which undertook the second voyage to the moon.

Meanwhile Amelia was taking an intensive course in meteorology under Dr. Kimball at the New York Weather Bureau and practicing blind flying whenever possible.

It was decided that Balchen would fly the plane up to Harbour Grace, Newfoundland, with a mechanic named Eddie Gorski and Amelia as passengers. Toward the middle of May Balchen and his crew had finished their work and nothing was holding up departure but the weather. A low-pressure area with heavy clouds and rain persisted in the eastern Atlantic. All Amelia could do was chafe and wait for the go signal from Dr. Kimball.

That the departure took place on May 20, 1932—five years to the day after Lindbergh soloed to Paris—was a coincidence dictated by the happenstance of weather conditions. In any case, there weren't the prolonged delays—or the emotional wear and tear—which had preceded the *Friendship* flight. And that was largely due to Bernt Balchen's efficient management of the preparatory stages of the venture.

Everything was set by May 18, except for the storm pattern which hovered over the eastern Atlantic. On May 19 the low-pressure area still hadn't moved. On the morning of May 20, with Putnam standing by at the New York Weather Bureau, Amelia left the house in Rye and drove over to the Teterboro Airport, determined to be on hand if they got clearance from Dr. Kimball. She arrived about 11:30 A.M. and was looking over the plane when Eddie Gorski came out and announced there was a call for her on the hangar phone.

Putnam was on the line with the news that Dr. Kimball, after looking over the latest reports from land stations and ships at sea, believed the route up the northeastern coast was clear enough for the flight.

"All the way to Newfoundland?" she asked.

"At least as far as St. John's," Putnam replied, "and probably all the way to Harbour Grace. A high-pressure area is moving down on Newfoundland."

"Okay, we'll go this afternoon," Amelia said without hesitation. "I'll see Bernt and we'll take off as soon as possible."

No good-byes, Amelia didn't believe in them. After a hasty conference with Balchen, it was decided they would take off at 3 P.M., which gave Amelia time to drive back to Rye and pick up her well-seasoned leather jacket and jodhpurs. She made it back to the airport at 2:55. Twenty minutes later, with Balchen at the controls, Gorski in the cockpit beside him, and Amelia lying on the cabin floor behind the extra fuel tank, they roared down the runway at Teterboro and headed for Canada.

Amelia slept most of the way, the flight to St. John's taking three hours and forty minutes. After an overnight stay in St. John's, they flew on to Harbour Grace, Newfoundland, the next day. A detailed weather report had been telegraphed from New York giving the go-ahead.

Amelia had been resting at a hotel in town when the

telegram from Putnam arrived. Balchen called her and in his matter-of-fact way suggested that she take off immediately for the other side of the Atlantic. Everything was done with dispatch. While she was being driven out to the airstrip, Balchen was drawing up a flight plan and Gorski was tuning up the engine.

Her traveling gear was as Spartan as the manner of her takeoff. Not even a dress for the receptions which would await her if the flight was a success. The only food she brought was a Thermos bottle of soup and a can of tomato juice, punctured, with a straw inserted. "A pilot whose land plane falls into the Atlantic"—her Lockheed was equipped with wheels rather than floats—"is not consoled by caviar sandwiches," she had reflected before the flight. "Everything but the bare essentials would distract my attention from the main object."

She took off with sunset lingering on the lakes and tundra behind her. When the moon came up as she arrowed eastward over the calm sea, it was partly concealed by clouds. She had climbed to 12,000 feet, then leveled off for what looked like a smooth progress over the North Atlantic.

Then her luck began a turn for the worse. First it was the altimeter: The hand on the dial began swinging around; it was obviously out of commission.

And with incredible swiftness the weather turned against her. One moment she was sailing through a moonlit sky. The next, clouds were blotting out the moon. A few minutes later her plane was being buffeted by what she hoped was only a patch of storm. Instead she had to ride out almost an hour of rain and lightning. Catching a glimpse of the moon through layers of cloud, she decided to try climbing above the storm. Trouble was, she had no way of knowing just how high she was with the altimeter broken. Too high and she'd start picking up ice on the wings, which could be fatal in a day when deicing equipment had not been developed.

The feel of the plane was all wrong, the controls were sluggish, and she wasn't climbing as fast as she should.

Then she spotted the telltale sign of slush on the windshield. The tachometer, which registered the motor's revolutions per minute and told her how much power she was using, had picked up ice and started spinning the hand on the dial.

From then on, she had to fight her way every mile of the storm-tossed hours around midnight. If she were able to look out on the wings, she knew, they would be coated with ice. The only course was to fly lower and let the ice melt off. Fog at a lower altitude would forward the melting process. At the same time she knew it was dangerous, given their dubious accuracy, to trust her instruments—those still operating—and fly blind.

She brought the plane down so low, in fact, that she caught a glimpse of the waves breaking through the fog layers beneath her. Even she must have known a split second of panic. Hastily she hauled back on the controls, gunned the engine, and brought the plane up to a safer level.

As she later described that moment, which had brought her very close to the end of everything, she had gone into a spin while descending and almost lost control of the plane. "I carried a barograph, an instrument which records on a disc the course of a plane, its rate of ascent and descent, its levels of flight all coordinated with clocked time. My telltale disc could tell a tale. At one point it recorded an almost vertical drop of 3,000 feet. It started at an altitude of something over 3,000 feet, and ended—well, something above the water. That happened when the plane suddenly iced up and went into a spin. How long we spun I do not know. I do know that I tried my best to do exactly what one should do with a spinning plane, and regained flying control as the warmth of the lower altitude melted the ice. As we righted and held level again, through the blackness below I could see the whitecaps too close for comfort."

She had passed the point of no return, and there was nothing to do but press on through the heavy overcast. Trust the gyrocompass and hope it would guide her to a landfall. If the Wasp engine kept functioning, she had a fair chance of making it.

The clouds thinned somewhat as the night wore on. Occasionally she would catch a glimpse of a star. Hour after hour she crouched in the cockpit, hands gripping the controls, eyes glued to the instrument panel or peering through the windshield. Every fifteen minutes she had to set the Sperry gyrocompass to a new heading. The only food she took was the can of tomato juice, at which she sipped from time to time. Opening the Thermos of soup would have been too much trouble.

Mechanically, the Lockheed functioned well. There was a flicker of alarm when she noticed flames shooting out through a crack in the exhaust manifold, but it was made of heavy metal, and she believed it would last until the flight was over. If it did splinter and break off, however, the flight would end very suddenly.

At first light she found herself flying between two layers of cloud, one above her at about 20,000 feet, the other below her and apparently hugging the surface of the sea. Ten hours had passed since takeoff. The sunlight was blinding, and she had to slip on a pair of dark glasses.

Far below she glimpsed a ship, possibly an oil tanker, through the lower layer of clouds.

The exhaust manifold had begun vibrating badly, indicating it wouldn't last much longer. The nearest land, if her navigation had been fairly precise, was Ireland. If the flight had been smoother, she would have liked to land in Paris, à la Lindbergh, but that was out of the question now. The northern Irish coast was her best bet. She set the compass on a new heading, due east, because the wind most of the night had been from the northwest and might have blown her slightly off course.

An intense weariness, the result of flying from sunset to dawn, and now beyond, under the most tense and trying conditions, had taken a grip on her.

There was a humped shape, slowly assuming a sharper definition, through the haze ahead. Land. The hills of Donegal. A thunderstorm was lashing the eastern coast of Ireland, and she decided to turn north out of fear of plowing into the mountains. The gleaming line of a railroad—the pioneer aviator's best friend—ran up the coast. She followed it, hoping it would lead to a city large enough to have an airport. A city she later learned was Londonderry appeared below; she circled, looked for an airport, didn't find one, and decided to come down on the most promising of the meadows around the city.

"I succeeded in frightening all the cattle in the county, I think," she said later, "as I came down low several times before finally landing in a long, sloping meadow." It was a smooth landing. She cut the switch and locked on the brakes. Her watch told her that she had flown from Harbour Grace to Londonderry in fifteen hours and eighteen minutes—more than five hours faster than the *Friendship* flight.

A farmer came clumping over the pasture in his Wellingtons and stared open-jawed into the cockpit.

Amelia grinned and said, "I've come from America."

"Have you now?" Dan McCallion asked. His employer, Patrick Gallagher, and several dairymaids came running up to be similarly astonished. Gallagher borrowed a neighbor's car and took her to a house a half-dozen miles down the road where there was a telephone. She managed to put through a transatlantic call to George Putnam in New York and tell him where she had landed. Then she went back to Gallagher's farm home and slept through the afternoon and night.

When she awakened that Sunday morning, she found the world outside those green Irish hills clamoring to embrace her. Paramount News had dispatched a plane to the Londonderry airport to bring her to London.

Putnam caught the next liner to join his wife and

share, a bit eagerly perhaps, in the spotlight. Amelia was put through the lionizing process with which she was now wearily familiar—award ceremonies, luncheons, dinners, receptions.

The White House, on their return to America, could not be outdone. Amelia and her husband were guests of President and Mrs. Herbert Hoover—a cheerless stay because the President was preoccupied by the worsening Depression and, unlike crowned heads, had to worry about the forthcoming election. Nevertheless Hoover spoke with more than usual warmth when he presented Amelia with the gold medal of the National Geographic Society at a full-dress affair in Constitution Hall.

"Her success," President Hoover declared, "has not been won by the selfish pursuit of a purely personal ambition, but as part of a career generously animated by a wish to help others to share in the rich opportunities of life, and by a wish also to enlarge those opportunities by expanding the powers of women as well as men to their ever-widening limits."

Amelia made her low-keyed and modest reply that "the appreciation for the deed is out of proportion to the deed itself." No doubt she believed it. If she was a pioneer of the air age, there were other frontiers to be crossed.

CHAPTER 11

AN ADDITION OF LAURELS

THERE IS SOMETHING ADDICTIVE ABOUT GLORY. If Amelia Earhart had an outsized ego, she concealed it well; yet she was always preoccupied with breaking new records, racking up new achievements. Something would not let her rest; something pushed her on to risk her life, time after time, in search of new conquests.

Only three months after flying the Atlantic she established the women's nonstop transcontinental speed record, Los Angeles to New York in nineteen hours and five minutes. Eleven months later she broke her own record over the same course, flying it in seventeen hours and seven minutes.

Amelia and her husband were also taken up socially by the new First Family: Franklin and Eleanor Roosevelt. Amelia and Eleanor Roosevelt were sympathetic because both had been social workers, both shared something of the same do-good spirit, and both regarded themselves as ugly duckling types.

Amelia, in fact, almost made Eleanor Roosevelt the First Flying First Lady.

The first intimation that the President's wife might, under Amelia's encouragement, be taking wing came in a story published by the *Washington Post:* "A slim, quiet woman in a white evening dress took Mrs. Roosevelt on a flight over Washington and Baltimore last night, piloting the big transport plane without even removing her long white kid gloves."

Amelia and her husband had dined at the White House that night, and later Amelia told Mrs. Roosevelt about the peculiar fascination of flying at night, the sense of freedom, the communion with the starlit heavens. Noting that the adventurous First Lady was intensely interested in her description of night flying, Amelia impulsively asked her, "Would you like to try it?"

"Tonight?" Mrs. Roosevelt said.

"Why not?"

Without telling her own husband or Mrs. Roosevelt's,

Amelia arranged to borrow a plane from Eastern Airlines. They sped out to the National Airport and took off with Amelia at the controls, Mrs. Roosevelt in the copilot's seat, several newspaperwomen and Mrs. Roosevelt's brother Hall back in the cabin.

Mrs. Roosevelt decided that she'd like to learn to fly herself—as privately as possible—with Amelia as her instructor. As required by law, she took a complete medical examination from a friend of Amelia's, Dr. Harry Templeton Smith. Mrs. Roosevelt then wrote Amelia: "I am enclosing my student pilot permit. Dr. Smith seemed to feel that I was all right. The question now comes as to whether I can induce my husband to let me take lessons. I will let you know if I am successful with him. I haven't had a chance even to talk to him about it."

Mrs. Roosevelt was a strong-minded woman who had her own way about a lot of things, but the President firmly quashed that project.

In 1934 Amelia was planning a flight from Hawaii to California, a venture which had been attempted by other pilots but never successfully. She would have to cross 2,400 miles of the Pacific. The lure, in part, was the $10,000 prize put up by a group of Hawaiian businessmen.

She sold her old Lockheed Vega, in which she had flown the Atlantic, and bought a new plane of the same make, similarly painted red to attract any air-sea rescue mission if she had to make a forced landing.

For the months preceding the flight she and her husband moved out to their Hollywood base. She had engaged as her technical adviser, navigational instructor, and engineering consultant the thirty-one-year-old Paul Mantz, who operated a small fleet of planes which he stunted for films. Mantz was a Hollywood swashbuckler, a handsome, hard-living fellow who looked as much like an actor as any of those he impersonated.

Aside from their German ancestry and their profession, two people could hardly have had less in common than Amelia Earhart and Paul Mantz. He was a professional daredevil, but he was also a highly skilled and scientific pilot, and Amelia respected that.

Just before Christmas, accompanied by Mantz and her husband, Amelia sailed for Honolulu aboard the Matson liner SS *Lurline.* Her plane was covered with a tarpaulin and lashed to the liner's forward deck. Reporters who greeted her when the ship docked wanted to know whether she was going to attempt the Hawaii-California flight, but Amelia refused to disclose her plans. Her passion for secrecy, her almost superstitious belief that talking about a project in advance tended to jinx it, particularly if it was broadcast in the newspapers, was still unyielding.

Her closely watched preparations for the flight, however, made it apparent that she would attempt the California flight. She had to wait for the right weather conditions and for the go-ahead from Paul Mantz, who was testing the new Lockheed and all its engineering and navigational equipment.

On January 11, 1935, she was all set for the takeoff, provided there was a break in the weather. It was squally around the islands that morning. At noon Amelia took a nap while her husband and Mantz consulted with the Navy's weather experts. At 3:30 the letter advised the flight's managers that there would be good weather along the projected course to California, but she'd have to take off before a line storm moved in from the west. If she delayed, Lieutenant E. W. Stevens of the meteorological office warned, she might be held up another ten days by a procession of tropical storms moving in from the central Pacific.

"Let's go, then," was Amelia's decision after listening to the weather forecast.

She drove out to Wheeler Field from the house at Waikiki where she had been a guest. The field was muddy from recent downpours. The Lockheed was heavily loaded but had a 6,000-foot runway for the takeoff. The 500 gallons of extra gasoline, the radio equipment, and other navigational aids brought the plane's weight up to three tons and over and would make it awkward to lift off the muddy runway.

At 4:30 P.M. she began to roll down the runway, laboriously gathered speed, struggled to get off the ground, and slowly began to lift. The worst part, Amelia thought, was over. She climbed to 5,000 feet and passed over Diamond Head, then gained another 2,000 feet of altitude. At least she wouldn't have to worry about fog or ice clogging her wings on this flight.

And the radio was functioning perfectly. As she flew through clear, starlit skies, she maintained radio contact with Hawaiian stations at half-hour intervals. With the map on her knees, she checked the position of various ships along her course, which were supposed to turn on their searchlights if they heard her passing overhead. By midnight she was 900 miles out from Wheeler Field.

The Matson liner *Maliko* spotted her, turned on her searchlight, was answered by blinking from the Lockheed's landing lights, and radioed the plane's position to Honolulu. In the early-morning hours she was entertained by snatches of a broadcast of the San Francisco Symphony Orchestra. The engine was functioning perfectly; the weather was holding clear, and she celebrated with a postmidnight supper of malted milk tablets and hot chocolate from a Thermos bottle.

Just after sunrise Amelia spotted a large passenger ship 8,000 feet below. Circling it several times, she learned it was the Dollar liner *President Pierce,* San Francisco-bound from Honolulu. She lined up her plane with the ship's mile-long wake and learned that her navigation through the night via compass had been absolutely accurate.

By radio she contacted radio station KPO in San Francisco and learned that the *President Pierce* was just 300 miles off the California coast.

Shortly before noon she sighted the coastal mountains of California, turned north, and caught a glimpse of the waters of San Francisco Bay. A few minutes later she was touching down at the Bay Farm Island Airport near Oakland. The flight from Honolulu had taken eighteen hours and fifteen minutes—and it was a real first for any flier, male or female. Ten thousand people, having been alerted by newspaper and radio reports of her progress, were waiting to cheer and mob her. It was the longest flight she had ever made, and she was somewhat surprised to find herself wobbling from weariness when she jumped out of the plane. She managed to give the crowd the expected Earhart grin, then a large police escort opened a path to the waiting car and a round-the-clock sleep.

CHAPTER 12

LOS ANGELES TO MEXICO CITY TO NEWARK

AMELIA'S MODESTY WAS UNDIMINISHED BY the praise raining down on her for the Pacific flight. Nothing embarrassed her more than excessive praise or irritated her more than an undeserved compliment. She kept a file labeled BUNK for hymns to her valor and messages of fulsome flattery which she regarded as making her seem ridiculous by going too far.

Along with that inherent modesty went the compulsion to accept any challenge that presented itself in the field of aviation. Only three months after the Pacific flight she was winging her way solo from Los Angeles to Mexico City, another first. Lindbergh of course had flown from Washington to Mexico City in 1927. The idea for the flight came from the President of Mexico—the first time a government had invited her. The challenge came from the veteran flier Wiley Post, who had become a friend of hers, although he didn't mean it as a dare.

Discussing the proposed Mexican flight with Post, she explained that she intended to fly to the Mexican capital from Los Angeles, then from Mexico City to Newark. On the return flight she would use the most direct route, across the Gulf of Mexico.

"That's about seven hundred miles," he protested. "Almost half an Atlantic. How much time do you lose if you go around by the shore?"

"About an hour," she replied.

"Amelia, don't do it," he said earnestly. "It's too dangerous."

Amelia said later she could hardly believe her ears. "Did Wiley Post, the man who had braved every sort of hazard in his stratosphere flying, really regard a simple little flight from Mexico City to New York across the Gulf as too hazardous? If so, I could scarcely wait to be on my way." What may really have made her determined to make the flight was the reflection that Post considered the flight too dangerous *for a woman*; that would make it a challenge indeed. If her aerial exploits were to some extent compulsive, it was because she felt it necessary to prove a woman could earn and hold her place in a man's world, and there was no more masculine sphere of influence than flying.

The Mexico City flight was one more attempt at proving that women had earned the right to take the controls of the latest aircraft and use the most advanced equipment.

Once again she favored night flying, perhaps more because of its poetic than its practical aspects.

Amelia loved flying at night, alone with the stars, and had done so on both the Atlantic and Hawaii-California flights. On the flight from Burbank, California, to Mexico City she took off shortly before midnight on April 19, 1935. The moonscape over the Southwest did not disappoint her. Later she wrote of a "generous moon which gilded the hills gloriously. . . . Even the mechanical difficulties which beset the early hours of the flight—chiefly an engine which overheated because of a faulty propeller setting—could not mar the rare loveliness of the night and of the farflung countryside which slumbered beneath."

During the early stage of the flight, while negotiating the Gulf of California, Amelia was troubled by a white haze which made it difficult to differentiate between the water and the horizon. Her engine overheated, but she managed to correct that by resetting the propeller.

Otherwise the flight proceeded smoothly, and she was on target reaching Mazatlán, her checkpoint, about a thousand miles from the Burbank airport. At Mazatlán, according to her chart, she was to turn east and fly over the high plateaus and the mountains of central Mexico to the capital. From an altitude of 10,000 feet she spotted the towns of Guadalajara and Tepic. The morning hours droned by. Her estimated time of arrival at Mexico City was about 1 P.M. Mexican time.

When that hour passed and there was no sign of Mexico City, she became somewhat concerned: She had to find out where she was, so she picked out what looked like a level place and descended. It turned out to be a dry lakebed, dotted with cactus and prickly pear. Within minutes after her plane rolled to a stop, men on horseback came out from the nearby village. There was a language barrier; she couldn't speak Spanish, and the horsemen couldn't speak English. She showed her map to a bright-looking youth, and they made out through sign language. Pointing to the map, he indicated she had landed outside the village of Nopala. Mexico City was about fifty miles away.

Half an hour later she landed at the airport outside the capital and was given an enthusiastic welcome.

As it turned out, she had to spend eight days in Mexico City before receiving the telegraphed go-ahead from her friend, Dr. Kimball, in the New York Weather Bureau. Meanwhile, the Mexican army was clearing a three-mile runway for her heavily loaded plane on the mud flats of what had once been the bottom of Lake Texcoco outside Mexico City.

She received the favorable weather bulletin shortly after midnight on May 8 and decided to make the return flight immediately. Driving at once out to Lake Texcoco, she watched while drums of gasoline were poured into her Lockheed's tanks; for her own sustenance her Mexican friends had provided enough food for a dozen flights: hard-boiled eggs, sandwiches, tomato juice, and a Thermos of coffee. A Pan American Airways mechanic gave her engine its final checkup under the headlights of an automobile parked as close to the cowling as possible.

For all of Wiley Post's forebodings, this was the least troubled of all her long-distance flights. Her engine drumming steadily, she flew over Tampico, then headed northeast over the Gulf of Mexico to New Orleans. She was in constant radio communication with the ground stations.

Crossing the 700-mile stretch of water, she later recorded, she first thought of the possibility of using a larger, two-engined plane. There was nothing but blue water from horizon to horizon, and "one's imagination toyed with the thought of what would happen if the single engine of the Lockheed Vega should conk. Not that my faithful Wasp ever had failed me, or indeed, even protested mildly. . . . On that sunny morning out of the sight of land, I promised my lovely red Vega I'd fly her across no more water. And I promised myself that any further over-ocean flying would be attempted in a plane with more than one motor, capable of keeping aloft with a single engine. Just in case. . . ."

This flight, however, went off with a "delightful precision." From New Orleans she followed her flight plan up the line to Mobile, Atlanta, Charlotte, Richmond, Washington. When she passed over Washington, her old friend Gene Vidal was standing by at the ground station and told her by radio, "You've done enough. You'd better land at Hoover Airport."

"No, thanks," Amelia replied. "I'm going through to New York."

Thousands, including her husband and Dr. Kimball, were waiting to greet her when she landed, fourteen hours and nineteen minutes after taking off from Mexico

City, at Newark Airport. The crowd overflowed the field and mobbed her plane before she could wearily clamber out of the cockpit. The painful aspect of mass adulation soon presented itself. A flying wedge of policemen forced its way to her rescue. One police officer had her by the right arm, another had taken a firm grip on her left leg, and Amelia became the victim of a tug-of-war.

For a few minutes, she said, she knew "the fleeting taste of the tortures of the rack" until her rescuers sorted themselves out and hauled her through the screaming mob and into a police car. Now she could appreciate some of Lindbergh's feelings about idolatrous crowds, who sometimes seemed to be looking for a blood sacrifice, but she took care not to show it.

During the latter part of 1935 Amelia decided to seek a more secluded and less active life for a time. She needed time and peace of mind to decide what her next move would be. Even while flying up from Mexico earlier in the year, part of her mind had been focused on the possibility of circumnavigating the earth in a multi-engined plane. The chanciness of further and riskier ventures, balanced against her ambitions, also had to be taken into consideration.

CHAPTER 13

CRACK-UP IN HAWAII

AMELIA BEGAN PREPARING HERSELF FOR ONE last great effort—the greatest challenge in aviation at the time. She would fly around the world.

Behind that project, as Amelia avowed, there was a sober scientific purpose. She proposed to make a "human guinea pig" of herself and "test human reactions" to long-distance flights.

Preparations, she believed, were responsible for two-thirds of the success of any long and dangerous flight. So she prepared with greater diligence than ever before for the round the world venture; to the flier it represented what Mount Everest did to the mountain climber. The late Wiley Post had flown around the world twice in his Lockheed Vega in 1931 and 1933. In 1935 he and Will

Rogers set out for Post's third flight around the world, which ended when his nose-heavy Lockheed Orion crashed into the Alaskan tundra and killed both men.

Amelia's project, however, was more daring. While Post's flights had been made north of the equator, Amelia's would circle the earth roughly *at* the equator, a much longer distance of about 27,000 miles. The route she originally laid out was east to west, from Oakland to Honolulu to Howland Island in the central Pacific to Port Darwin in northern Australia, then from Australia to Africa via Arabia, across the South Atlantic to Brazil, and back to the United States.

Obviously she would need a navigator, one who knew celestial navigation, who could guide her across long trackless stretches of ocean. On her previous flights she had "dead-reckoned" her way to landfall, but "then I was aiming at continents, not small spots of land in the mightiest ocean."

And there were other preparations which had to be made long before she took off on the first leg of the flight. Her husband was in charge of most of these. He arranged with Standard Oil to have gasoline cached around the whole route of her flights and with Pratt & Whitney for spare parts wherever they might be needed. Putnam also had to obtain clearances from the embassies of the various countries where she would land or which she would fly over to avoid any charges of aerial trespassing. A small corps of experts was working on various other problems. Paul Mantz again was the technical adviser (at a fee of $100 a day), and Clarence S. Williams of Los Angeles prepared all the maps and charts she would need.

Money was getting to be a problem, as Putnam wrote Mantz. "It may interest you to know," he added, "that it looks as if the airlines, jointly and entirely on their own, are going to do something for AE. They seem to recognize her as the most important single agency in America today popularizing air travel. Especially combatting feminine sales resistance. Which would be nice and fair enough, if it comes through. As usual, she is asking for nothing."

Mantz, however, had plenty to worry about in the mechanical line and was particularly concerned about the problem of pilot fatigue. With all his respect for Amelia's capabilities, he wasn't at all certain that a woman could stand up to the long hours of staying at the controls during a globe-girdling flight. "A Sperry Robot Pilot," he wrote Putnam, "is essential; it will eliminate fifty percent of her fatigue." He also insisted that her instrumental flying must be more precise and disciplined. He installed a Link blind-flying trainer, which simulated the actual conditions of flight in a closed cockpit, in his Burbank hangar for endless hours of putting Amelia through her paces.

At the end of 1936 Mantz was fairly satisfied with the plane and confident of its performance but admittedly was worried about pilot fatigue and navigation. He wondered whether Amelia was in prime condition, considering the fact that she had delivered 136 lectures that year, among all her other activities. He worried about whether she was being pushed too far too fast. Navigating a plane around the world took a combination of skills which few men possessed.

For navigation, celestial and otherwise, Captain Harry Manning who had been awarded the Congressional Medal of Honor for rescuing thirty-two passengers at sea, had volunteered to accompany the flight. On the first leg from Oakland to Australia they would have the services of Fred Noonan, who had been a Pan American Airways pilot and navigator and who would relieve Amelia at the controls over the longer stretches of ocean flying and also help Captain Manning with the navigation.

Early in 1937 everything seemed to be ready. Amelia had trained like an athlete and her mechanical experts had tuned the Lockheed Electra to the top pitch of performance.

On February 11, at a press conference summoned by her husband in the Hotel Barclay in New York, she announced her plans for the global flight. She was dressed in a dark blue woolen dress with a scarf tied around her throat, and Captain Manning was at her side. "Well," she told the reporters, "I'm going to try to fly around the globe as near the equator as I can make it, east to west, about twenty-seven thousand miles." She traced her route on a globe while newsreel cameramen and newspaper photographers closed in to take their pictures.

"You know," she remarked with a slightly nervous laugh, "I feel you men have pushed me into this. You're the ones who have kept saying and saying that I was going to fly around the world until finally you've compelled me to think seriously about doing it."

She was kidding, of course, but one of the reporters snapped at the bait. "Oh, come on now," he said, "nobody has pushed you into it. You know you've been wanting to do it all the time."

Amelia grinned and replied, "Yes, I suppose you're right. I didn't get away with it, did I?"

A certain amount of controversy arose over the flight and over all such attempts to expand man's mastery over the planet. Some of her closest friends in aviation were dubious about the merits of her flight plan and about her plane's ability to negotiate such long distances over water.

Aside from her friends' reactions and doubts and pre-monitions, a certain amount of public resistance was cropping up. So many lives had been lost in aerial adventures that seemed, on reflection, to prove nothing but the extent of human self-confidence. Even those who made a career of flying were having their doubts about the heroic age of aviation.

With Amelia, nothing counted but the flight itself. Nothing but bad weather or mechanical difficulties would stand in her way. On March 17, 1937, she and the plane and her crew were ready for takeoff. The crew on the first hop from Oakland to Honolulu now included Captain Manning, Fred Noonan, and Paul Mantz, who wanted to visit his fiancée in Hawaii and who would act as copilot. Rain kept falling until about 4:30 P.M. The skies then cleared, and the Lockheed Electra was towed out of a Navy hangar.

Amelia, driven to the head of the 7,000-foot runway in a Navy staff car, took over the controls with Mantz beside her in the cockpit. Manning and Noonan were in the cabin behind them.

The Electra roared down the runway and easily lifted its five tons into the air with 4,000 feet of runway to spare. The landing gear was retracted. Amelia took it up to 2,000 feet and then leveled off as they headed over the Golden Gate and out over the Pacific. Their departure had been kept secret, except for a San Francisco *Chronicle* photographer who had been tipped off, had rented a small plane, and got a striking picture of the Electra passing over the Golden Gate Bridge which made front pages all over the country the next morning.

The flight was so smooth, so uneventful, that if any of the participants were superstitious, they would, like actors, have feared the portents of an untroubled dress rehearsal. Just eight minutes short of sixteen hours later they landed at Wheeler Field, near Honolulu.

Along the way Mantz, sharing the cockpit with her, had coached Amelia on reducing her power settings so the Electra cruised at a true airspeed of 150 miles an hour and burned 38 gallons of gasoline an hour. Mantz later reported that in the past he had "found that Amelia had a tendency to push her engines to the limit, flying with extra power to make up for headwinds. . . . I had to convince her of the danger of this method on critical long-range flights." He also was perturbed because she looked "groggy" at the end of the flight and asked him to land the plane at Wheeler. "I just took a reading on the radio compass—Makapuu Point was dead ahead," Mantz recalled.

"I stuck the nose down and started the letdown, through the undercast. It was just about dawn, and we could see the glow of lights. I went around Makapuu Point and then crossed Wheeler Field. I wrapped it around in a steep bank to check the wind sock. AE yelled 'Don't! Don't!' She was very fatigued and kind of exuberant. She calmed down when I made a normal approach pattern and we landed. . . ."

From Hawaii, after dropping Mantz and refueling, they would make the long leap over the central Pacific to tiny Howland Island, an American possession, where the government had recently built an emergency landing field. The Coast Guard vessel *Itasca* would be standing by to render any necessary assistance.

For the next takeoff, which was dependent on a weather clearance, the Electra was flown over to Luke Field near Pearl Harbor. Amelia wanted to leave almost immediately, after a few hours' rest, but a storm was spotted moving in from the southwest.

The departure was put off until the morning of March 20, which gave Amelia a full day of sunbathing and relaxation at Waikiki Beach.

Next day everything looked fine for the takeoff, but as she observed, "When things are going very well is just the time to anticipate trouble." Mantz had preceded them to

Luke Field to warm up the plane and inspect the fuel, which was commercial gasoline brought over by tank truck. A good thing he did. He found water and sediment in the fuel and hustled up a new supply. Using his charm on the commanding officer of the Hawaiian Air Depot, he managed to buy 590 gallons of the new high-test military aviation fuel.

Amelia, along with Captain Manning and Fred Noonan, climbed into the Electra just as first light was touching the hills to the east of Pearl Harbor.

There were 3,000 feet of concrete runway, with patches of sea visible beyond. As soon as the Electra began trundling down the strip, Amelia knew something was wrong; the plane was sluggish in answering the throttle. It was loaded with 900 gallons of gasoline, more than enough for the flight to Howland, but Amelia had insisted that because of uncertainty about the weather ahead they must have enough fuel to return to Luke after eight flying hours.

Halfway down the runway she knew they were in a May Day situation. The plane wasn't getting up enough speed for liftoff. Suddenly it lurched to the left. The corrective measures Amelia took immediately—throttling back on the left engine—caused the plane to career into a wide circle and then ground-loop. The right landing wheel was sheared off and the right wing badly damaged.

Only the sturdiness of Lockheed construction, she said later, prevented a complete wipeout of the ship.

Amelia kept her head even as the plane was going out of control. She cut the switches before it came to a stop and thereby prevented a spark from setting off the gasoline which poured from the ruptured wing tank. None of the plane's occupants was hurt, but it was apparent that the Electra would never fly again unless it was sent back to the mainland for a factory overhaul.

Fire engines raced out to the crippled plane, with Mantz aboard one of them. Amelia had just jumped to the ground, following Manning and Noonan, when Mantz came up. "I don't know what happened, Paul," she told him.

Mantz had warned her against "jockeying" the throttles on takeoff, and he believed that was what had caused the trouble. "That's all right," he said, putting his arm around her. "So long as nobody was hurt. You just didn't listen to Papa, did you?"

The Electra was dismantled, hauled to the Honolulu docks, and sent back to Burbank for repairs.

Mantz's opinion was that the plane would be airworthy in "a couple of months."

There were differing opinions on what caused the crackup. There was Mantz's that throttle-jockeying was to blame. Some witnesses on the ground said one of the tires blew out, but Amelia studied the tracks on the runway and concluded that this could not have been the primary cause. Some alleged that Amelia had simply lost control of the heavily loaded plane. Others guessed that the extra gasoline had been improperly loaded and had unbalanced the ship. Amelia herself came to no definitive verdict but believed the right shock absorber on the landing gear may have given way.

She refused to give up on the project. Even as the Electra was slithering down the runway with sparks flying and metal crunching, she said later, she thought to herself, "If we don't burn up, I want to try again."

CHAPTER 14

THE OTHER WAY AROUND

WITH THE FAILURE AT HONOLULU, AMELIA and her advisers had to recast their plans completely. More money had to be raised for rebuilding parts of the Electra. Gasoline and spare-parts caches had to be rearranged, since it was decided that Amelia would fly west to east on the second attempt; later in the spring the weather patterns, according to meteorologists, made that reversal advisable.

Everything had to be done in a crash program to get the flight started no later than early June; actually, it took off two weeks earlier than that, thanks to a rush job done on the Electra at the Lockheed factory in Burbank.

Psychologically she was unaffected by the near-disaster on Luke Field. She had always been a fatalist and more than once told her husband and friends that when she died, "I'd like to go in my plane." Putnam, looking back on their life together, would realize that "wholly without melodramatics" she could never visualize herself getting old; death would save her from that indignity. "It is hard to be old," she told him once. "I'm afraid I'd hate it."

Because of the delay Captain Manning, on leave of absence from his ship, had to drop out as navigator. Amelia decided that Fred Noonan would share her adventure. Aside from the fact that he could act as copilot as well as navigator, she liked the coolness he had shown when their plane cracked up in Hawaii. When the ground crew wrenched open the cabin door, she learned, they saw Noonan methodically folding up his charts, completely unrattled.

The tall, handsome, blue-eyed Irishman was a veteran of the world of adventure. Chicago-born, he had gone to sea at the age of seventeen and served on the British square-rigger *Compton*. During World War I he had served as an officer on a Royal Navy munitions ship and survived three torpedoings. He stayed in the merchant marine after the war until he became interested in aviation. With his experience as a navigator, he obtained a job with Pan American Airways, learned to fly, and served as both pilot and navigator on the airline's overseas flights. In 1935 he was detailed to map out the line's transpacific routes from San Francisco to Hawaii, Midway, Wake Island, Guam, the Philippines, and Hong Kong. When the first Pan Am China Clipper, a four-engined Martin flying boat, took off on the first Pacific flight, Noonan was aboard as navigator.

Amelia could hardly have found a man with more or better experience as her collaborator, but he had one flaw. It seemed to be the inevitable one in the men to whom Amelia in some measure entrusted her life: alcohol. First her father, then Bill Stultz, now Noonan, who was said to have acquired a two-bottles-a-day habit. He had a better head for the stuff than the senior Earhart or Stultz, and his associates said they never saw him incapacitated for duty because of drinking. Yet Pan Am had let him go as a bad risk.

The association with Amelia Earhart, in fact, constituted Noonan's comeback. He had sworn off the stuff. He was in love with a California girl named Mary Martinelli and married her on March 27, 1937, immediately after returning from the aborted Hawaii takeoff.

Even before they boarded ship for San Francisco, Amelia had more or less decided to take on Noonan as her navigator. She knew about his problem and was a total and understandably dedicated abstainer herself, but there was still enough of the social worker in her to believe in the possibility of rehabilitation.

After telling him Captain Manning would have to go back to his ship, she asked Noonan, "Do you feel up to staying with me?"

Noonan nodded. "I need this flight."

"I mean all the way," Amelia said, "as the only navigator. I've decided against even trying to make part of the flight alone."

"Do you trust me?" Noonan asked.

"I believe in you."

"Then," Noonan said, "I'll give you the best I have."

On May 17, less than two months after the Hawaiian crackup, the Electra had been repaired and rolled out of the Lockheed hangar. The plan was to fly the Electra to Miami, give it a final tuning up, then cross the thousand miles of Caribbean to Puerto Rico; then to Brazil, Africa, Karachi, Burma, Singapore, Australia, Howland Island, Hawaii, and back to Oakland.

Paul Mantz was furious when he heard the news that Amelia had begun the round-the-world venture so suddenly.

Mantz had urged that before Amelia flew the Electra

from Burbank again there be a final check of its radio equipment (whose functioning still didn't satisfy him), a rehearsal of the power settings that would get the most mileage out of the fuel supply, and more rest and seclusion.

For the next week Amelia and the others waited in Miami while a corps of Pan Am experts went over the Electra at the airline's terminal, making final adjustments to the engines and instruments.

On June 1 Amelia rose before dawn and drove out to the Miami municipal airport with her husband. Shortly after 5 A.M. she and Noonan took their places in the cockpit; Putnam leaned in from the cabin to say good-bye, as briefly as possible, in accordance with Amelia's aversion to sentimental farewells, and then he and his son David joined the ground crew to watch the takeoff. The departure was conducted with her usual dispatch. At 5:56 A.M. the Electra took wing into the unclouded sky.

That was her farewell, unknowingly, of course, to America.

The Electra was a hundred miles off the Florida coast, heading for San Juan, Puerto Rico, when the Miami radio station WQAM broke into its scheduled programming to report that Amelia Earhart had just taken off safely on the beginning of her round-the-world flight. It pleased her that she had managed to leave without any fuss, any throng at the airport, any swarm of newspaper people. She stayed tuned to the station, by prearrangement, to receive a weather summary prepared by Pan Am meteorologists.

While Amelia piloted, Noonan kept an eye out for islands, lighthouses, reefs, and other features of the seascape below by which they could check their course and speed. By 6:30 A.M. they passed over the Bahama Banks and half an hour later Andros Island, off which they could see a submerged wreck like an undersea shadow.

Amelia locked the ship into the newly installed automatic pilot; the gyroscopic automatic pilot had made distance flying "pretty sissy," she decided. Noonan was back at the chart table in the cabin and communicated with Amelia by clipping notes to the end of a bamboo pole. At noon, via this rudimentary intercom, he informed her they were slightly off course for San Juan and gave her a new compass heading. They touched down at San Juan about an hour later.

They returned to the airport before dawn the next morning to learn they would have to work out a new route. Amelia had intended to make Paramaribo, Dutch Guiana, on the next hop, but the runway was being repaired; they would have to reduce the weight of the plane and could take only enough gasoline to reach Caripito, Venezuela.

Caripito was an oil town in a jungle clearing, but it had a concrete runway and a well-equipped hangar owned jointly by Pan Am and Standard Oil. The following morning, June 3, they took off into dense rain clouds, bucking 148-mile-an-hour headwinds until they picked up the jungle-bordered Surinam River and followed its course to Paramaribo, the capital of Dutch Guiana, then a narrow-gauge railway, a thin scar in the dense growth, to the airport 25 miles outside town.

Their next destination was Fortaleza, Brazil, over a course that took them 370 miles over the open sea and 960 miles over Brazilian jungle. If anything went wrong, there was little likelihood of a successful forced landing either in the jungle or on the 180-mile lower delta of the Amazon.

Ten hours later they came down, almost exactly on target with Noonan's estimated time of arrival, at Fortaleza, on a broad sandy plain west of Point Mucuripe. The Pan Am facilities were first-rate, and Amelia decided to have the Electra's engines overhauled and its instruments checked by the airline's mechanics there rather than down the line at Natal, their jump-off for Africa. That meant a two-day layover, part of which Amelia spent shopping for a lightweight raincoat and a sun helmet and part studying the local sociology. "I went tourist," she also confessed, "and took pictures of burros loaded with produce and human beings."

On June 6 they ran down the coast to Natal and its international airport, used by various airlines as the point of departure for flights across the South Atlantic. For several years the French had been running a twice-weekly mail service to West Africa and had two weather-reporting station ships in the South Atlantic. The French helped with her flight plan and shared their weather information.

The first long ocean hop loomed—1,900 miles to Dakar, Senegal. They took off in darkness at 3:15 A.M. June 7, hoping to make an African landfall before evening.

CHAPTER 15

FOLLOWING THE EQUATOR

THE ELECTRA WAS LOADED WITH 900 GALLONS of gasoline, and Amelia and her navigator must have thought back to that aborted takeoff from Luke Field, when the plane somehow had balked at its heavy burden. And there were complications on the predawn takeoff from Brazil. The longer runway was lighted, but there was a crosswind blowing. There was a secondary runway which was shorter, grass-surfaced, and unlighted. They had to survey it, in fact, with flashlights and pick out shadowy landmarks to guide them when the plane lifted off.

Risky as it looked, the takeoff was easy, the Electra functioned perfectly, and soon they were out over the dark sea bucking the prevailing winds. The sky ahead began glowing, and Amelia reflected that this was the third time she had seen dawn over the Atlantic from an airplane.

The weather was much as the Air France meteorologist had predicted. A period of head winds of about 20 miles an hour, then a spell of the doldrums, then clouds would build up with a tropical suddenness and intensity. For a few minutes they rode out the heaviest rain Amelia had ever seen; it pounded so hard she could feel the plane trembling.

Later on she wrote, "Seven hundred and something to go . . . that's about the mileage between Burbank and Albuquerque. Seems long way off . . . long way too from radio beams and lighted airways . . . our flyers at home don't know how pampered they are. . . ."

The only flaw in the flight was a navigational error, and that was probably due to Amelia's insistence on establishing the fact that, though a female, she was in command. It was a rather dangerous procedure in a way; if you trusted a navigator enough to take him on, and particularly if his experience and skill were greater than your own, you should be bound by his advice.

It happened as they approached the thick haze over the jungled coast of West Africa. Noonan, back at his chart table in the cabin, sent a note via fishing pole to

Amelia in the cockpit: They should turn south at 3:36 P.M. for Dakar, their scheduled landing place, which he estimated was 79 miles away.

Amelia shook her head. Instead of a left turn, she believed they should turn north. "What put us north?" she scrawled at the bottom of Noonan's note, indicating she believed he had made a navigational error.

So she followed her own hunch, rather than Noonan's scientific calculations, and turned north.

Feminine intuition, on that occasion, proved to be a faulty navigational aid. A town with an airfield appeared on the horizon, and Amelia set the Electra down. It turned out to be St.-Louis, Senegal, French West Africa, instead of the larger base of Dakar. Fortunately Air France had fueling and servicing facilities available on the field. "The fault," she admitted, "was mine"—and thereafter she would be less likely to rely on her own hunches.

After an overnight stay in St.-Louis, they hopped up the coast to Dakar for a two-day layover while the plane was checked over and they studied the geography they would encounter on the next leg of their flight.

She and Noonan spent hours at the governor-general's mansion tracing a route almost due east across the continent. There would have to be an overnight stop at Gao, now part of Mali, which was a trans-Saharan transportation center, and another at Fort-Lamy, Chad, in what was then French Equatorial Africa. A distance of 4,350 miles across the continent would have to be made in four hops.

Shortly after dawn on June 10, equipped with Air France weather charts indicating barometric lows and possible tornadoes in their path, they took off for Gao, 1,140 miles in the interior across Senegalese jungle and then vast stretches of veld and desert. Flying over a desert was more difficult than over an ocean, Noonan wrote his wife, because most of the maps were inaccurate and misleading. "At points," he wrote, "no dependence at all could be placed on them." And there were few recognizable landmarks in the desert. Even so, their navigation was on target. "In all the distance I don't think we wandered off the course for half an hour, although there were times when I wouldn't have bet a nickel on the accuracy of our assumed position."

They landed at ancient Gao, with its seventh-century mosque and lopped-off pyramid, well before nightfall and found the 50-gallon drums of gasoline marked "Amelia Earhart" waiting in a corner of the hangar as had been arranged months before; the logistics system never let them down.

Fortified by a predawn breakfast of mushroom omelet

and hot chocolate they departed on the Gao–Fort-Lamy hop over central Africa. "Thousand mile hops" over Africa, she noted, were coming to "seem routine. One quickly becomes accustomed to the feeling that when places are separated by a paltry five hundred miles they may be considered practically neighbors."

They flew over the vast shallows of Lake Chad, almost as much swamp as lake, and landed at Fort-Lamy. When they jumped out of the cabin, they saw that the landing gear had buckled. A leak had developed in one of the shock absorbers—the first mechanical trouble they had experienced since leaving Miami a dozen days before. It took the small ground crew at Fort-Lamy until 1:30 P.M. the next day to pump up the shock absorber and fix the leak, so they made a shorter hop than planned to El Fasher in the Anglo-Egyptian Sudan.

Next day they flew the 500 miles of trackless waste between El Fasher and Khartoum. Amelia locked into the autopilot and amused herself by studying the map for that section of the flight, which had been prepared in California months before, and wishing she could drop down and visit such splendid-sounding places as Qala-en Hahl, Umm Shinayshin, Abu Seid, Idd el Bashir, Fazi, Marabia Abu Fas—though from the air there were no visible villages or oases.

At Khartoum, capital of the Sudan, they landed at an airdrome near the racetrack, waited for two hours while the Electra was being refueled and checked over, and then took off again for Massawa, Eritrea.

They flew high over the Eritrean mountains and landed at Massawa, on the Red Sea, which Amelia was somewhat disappointed to observe was actually blue.

At Massawa they descended into a steam bath, 120 degrees in the shade, and were guests of the Italian commander. There was a language barrier, but they managed to have the engine checked, the oil changed, the tanks refilled. They also refueled themselves when an officer asked if Amelia was hungry and she replied, "As hollow as a bamboo horse," an old childhood saying which her hosts had some difficulty in translating.

Next day they flew the 335 miles to Assab, southeast down the hot barren Eritrean coast. Assab was closer than Massawa to Karachi, at that time part of India, their next destination. It was a long flight over Saudi Arabia and the Arabian Sea, almost 2,000 miles, and they needed the longer runways at Assab to lift their heavily loaded plane. A large supply of gasoline had been stored at Assab. Furthermore, the flight had to be nonstop because the Arabians refused permission to land. At first they had even forbidden Amelia to fly over the peninsula but had relented enough to permit an overflight of the southern tip.

Well before daybreak they took off from Assab and followed a carefully plotted course. Not only Arab hostility to the whole venture but the desolation below and the poor chances of surviving a forced landing dictated the most cautious navigation and made that leg of their journey seem the most hazardous thus far. For those back in America who followed the progress of the flight with the most interest and personal concern, the Assab-Karachi hop was an anxious period for another reason. As Amelia learned later by telephone, it had been announced that she was flying direct from Massawa to Karachi, without the stayover at Assab, and her husband, relatives, and friends were worried about her being overdue in India.

The flight took them over the southern entrance to the Red Sea and the southeastern tip of Arabia. They flew over the British protectorate at Aden as a checkpoint, also intending to use it as a landing place if the plane wasn't functioning properly. From Aden they traveled up the southern Arabian coast, keeping a few miles off the mountains and deserts of the Hadhramaut, which looked to Amelia quite as inhospitable as the rulers of that territory. "Some regions," she noted, "looked as if mighty harrows had churned the tortured badlands into a welter of razor-back ridges, fantastic mountains and thirsty valleys barren of vegetation and devoid of life." Poor as their chances would be of surviving a forced landing, they carried a letter in Arabic, composed by two linguists in New York, which would inform any nomadic sheikhs below that they had come in peace and their overflight had been permitted by the king himself.

The Electra bore them swiftly across the Arabian Sea toward Karachi, on the coast of what is now Pakistan. Only a minor mechanical disturbance marred the flight: the manual-mixture control lever jammed, and the starboard engine was using too much fuel. Amelia had to reduce their speed in order to conserve fuel.

They landed at the Karachi airport at 7:05 P.M., thirteen hours and ten minutes after leaving Assab.

There would be a two-day stay in Karachi while the ground crew of Imperial Airways tuned up the Electra and Royal Air Force experts readjusted the instruments.

The Maharaja of Jodhpur invited Amelia to fly up to his palace 300 miles cross-country and land at his private airport, but Amelia opted for simpler pleasures during the Karachi stay. The most fun was camel riding. Along with Noonan, and other companions, she visited an oasis several miles outside Karachi on camelback. A camel, she found, was balkier at the controls than an airplane. "I climbed into the saddle swung between his two humps. It was a startling takeoff as we rose. A camel unhinges himself in the most extraordinary fashion. As his hindlegs unfold you are threatened with a nose-dive forward. Then with a lurch that can unhorse (I mean un-camel) the unwary, the animal's center section, so to speak, hoists into the air. It is reminiscent of the first symptoms of a flat spin. Camels should have shock absorbers."

On June 17 she and Noonan resumed the journey, taking off for Calcutta along a well-established airway 1,390 miles across the subcontinent. They flew over the sandstorms of the Sind desert, then high over mountains from which black eagles sortied. The eagles flew so close to the plane Amelia had "some very bad moments" wondering what would happen if an eagle tangled with a propeller. They passed over Allahabad, knew that the Taj Mahal was close by, but decided not to make any sightseeing detours. Past Allahabad they ran into heavy rain and tricky air currents which swept the plane up a thousand feet while Amelia struggled to keep the nose down.

The outer perimeter of gardens and paddy fields, then the jute mills, and finally the docks of Calcutta appeared on the horizon, and they came down at Dum Dum airdrome. The field was waterlogged, and they sent up a fountain of spray as they taxied toward the hangar. The monsoon was about to break, and that was one good reason not to linger any longer than necessary. "Arriving in mid-June," Amelia said, "we'd been warned the monsoons might fall upon us momentarily. But we hoped to squeeze through before they struck their stride." That ride through the squalls had given them a hint of the bad weather to come.

The lowering clouds and oppressive atmosphere which precedes the rainy season in India weighed on her as they dined early and prepared for an early start the next morning. She had diligently read up on the subject of monsoons and knew that from June to September the prevailing wind shifts to the southeast. Their course to Burma was southeasterly. That meant they would be bucking heavy rains and winds "full on our nose."

They were up before dawn the next morning and found Dum Dum drenched from an overnight rain. That meant a precarious takeoff, but the weather experts at the airdrome advised them not to wait for the field to dry off, that more rains were coming and would fall intermittently through the day.

To Amelia it seemed the Electra would never lift off as the plane trundled down the runway and the wet sticky soil clung to its wheels. There was a fringe of trees around the airport which their plane barely cleared with a scraping of the landing gear on the upper branches.

At first the flight to Akyab, Burma, where they planned to refuel before continuing to the Burmese capital of Rangoon for an overnight stop, went fairly smoothly. They passed over the endless rice-paddy country of the Ganges and Brahmaputra mouths, which steamed in the heat and humidity. They came down at Akyab, across the Burmese frontier, and just had time to admire the two gold-leafed pagodas from a distance while the Electra's tanks were being refilled. It was a tiny place in the Burmese jungle, but the airport served as a servicing and refueling stop for KLM, Imperial Airways, and Air France, all of them vigorously competing for the air transport business of southeast Asia.

The local weatherman's reports on conditions they would meet on the renewed flight to Rangoon included wind and rain in storm proportions. Almost as soon as they leveled off after leaving Akyab, they ran into a black wall of storm clouds. Head winds laden with rain battered the Electra. The monsoon rain slanted down so hard, Amelia later observed, that "it beat patches of paint off the leading edge of my plane's wings." They would have drowned in the cockpit, she thought, if it hadn't been watertight. One needed a flying submarine to make it through a monsoon storm.

Visibility was nil in the blinding downpour. The monsoon seemed to wall them in. They tried for two hours to find an opening. First they headed out to sea and flew just above the choppy surface of the Bay of Bengal. Then they turned inland, still looking for a hole in the storm, but they were afraid to fly low because of the danger of ramming into a hilltop. There was nothing left to do but attempt a return, flying blind all the way, to the Akyab airport.

And that was Fred Noonan's job. Amelia's respect for his talents as a navigator had been steadily increasing ever since she had overruled him, mistakenly, on the approach to West Africa. She knew that if she had tried to navigate as well as fly her plane, she would have been lost many times over Africa and Asia. This day, June 18, he was doubly a blessing, literally a lifesaver. "By uncanny powers," she related, "Fred Noonan managed to navigate us back to the [Akyab] airport, without being able to see anything but the waves beneath our plane. His comment was, 'Two hours and six minutes of going nowhere.' For my part, I was glad that our landing gear was retractable, lest it be scraped on trees or waves."

At Akyab the airport people said there probably would

not be a break in the monsoon weather for another three months. Amelia and Noonan spent the night in the Burmese town, determined to make up for the delay by flying all the way to Bangkok the next day. But the weather was even worse June 19. This time they went up to 8,000 feet, found the upper air just as thick as that below, and bulled their way through the buffeting winds. After about two hours of that, they decided to come down at Rangoon and call it a day.

Somewhere along the Irrawaddy River they descended into sunlight. There was a broad rice-growing plain below. Somehow they had found a hole in the monsoon. Another 50 miles along the river, dodging through alternate patches of rain and sun, they sighted the golden curlicues of the Shwe Dagon Pagoda in the distance. It gleamed in the sun and served as a beacon.

The American consul not only volunteered his hospitality for the night but provided a car and showed them the sights. Driving down Kipling's "road to Mandalay," Amelia remarked to Noonan that now she knew what Kipling meant by flying fishes in his poem. "That's what aviators are," she said, "when they're silly enough to go up during the monsoons."

The hop to Bangkok and Singapore the next day was easier than they had expected, though they had to climb through squalls to the 8,000-foot level to traverse the high mountains forming the border between Burma and Thailand. After refueling at the Bangkok airport, they took off immediately for Singapore, eager to make up for lost time, and followed a course across the Gulf of Siam, then down the east coast of the Malay Peninsula. For the first time in days they had clear visibility. On landing at Singapore, they found the American consul-general and his wife waiting to welcome them. "They had the courage to take us for the night," Amelia observed, "even after I explained our disagreeable habit of getting up at three in the morning and falling asleep immediately after dinner."

Their flight the next day, begun before the tropic dawn lit up the skies, took them down the archipelago to Bandung, Java. It was beautiful weather, with beautiful scenery below; coming down into the southern hemisphere they seemed to be entering a gentler world. They could let the autopilot take over and admire the tiny, palm-sprouting islands off the Sumatran and Javanese coasts.

Landing at Bandung up in the densely wooded mountains, they taxied straight into a KLM hangar, where arrangements had been made for a checkout of the engines. Amelia whiled away the time by driving up to the surrounding volcanic peaks, half an hour up the mountain roads from Bandung, and coming across an elderly volcanologist. She was always fascinated by specialists and learned that he was employed by the Dutch government to keep a constant watch on the craters, though there had not been an eruption for almost thirty years. Two dogs accompanying him on his daily inspection of the craters were also rated as government employees; they sniffed the volcanic gases and gave warnings which had saved their master's life several times.

Next day, June 24, they planned to make the long jump to Port Darwin, Australia, but when they appeared at the airport, they found that one of the instruments was malfunctioning. Hours of waiting passed while the technicians tinkered with the long-range navigational instruments. Because it was late in the day when they finally were able to board the plane, they decided to make a shorter hop to Surabaya. En route, Noonan reported that the instruments were still out of whack, so they returned to Bandung. A thorough overhaul was indicated.

Perhaps, it would seem in retrospect, that instrument failure was more ominous than it appeared to Amelia and her navigator.

Not overly concerned, however, they took an excursion to Batavia to visit friends of Noonan's while Dutch Air Force and KLM technicians worked on the adjustments. It wasn't until two days later, June 27, that the plane was pronounced fit for duty. This time they were less ambitious and planned to make an overnight stop at Koepang, on the southern tip of the island of Timor, where they could stay at a government resthouse. It took five hours to reach Koepang, with Noonan reporting the instruments in working order again. Timor is a grassy, windswept island without the lush vegetation of Java or Sumatra. The airport was really only an emergency landing field, without any ground crew or hangars. A stone fence had been built around the field to keep out the wild pigs. Except for a shed where drums of gasoline were stored, there were no buildings in which to shelter the Electra. A horde of natives came out from the village to watch, with considerable amusement, while the two fliers struggled to protect the engines and propellers with canvas covers against the nightly dampness.

The most perilous phases of their journey, the long flights over the Pacific, were coming up, and stripping the plane of every ounce of excess baggage was very much on their minds.

As one means of lightening the plane's burden, they packed their parachutes and sent them back to the States.

"A parachute," Amelia somberly noted, "would not help over the Pacific."

CHAPTER 16

LAST DAYS ON LAND

THE LAST THOUGHTS OF AMELIA EARHART, some of them a trifle foreboding, before she and Fred Noonan disappeared into the Pacific skies were contained in the continuing story she was sending back to New York. Later it would be edited by George Putnam and published as a book, *Last Flight,* with its abrupt termination.

Before that final leg of her journey, she was a weary, travel-worn woman, perhaps a lot more exhausted than her last accounts to New York would indicate. She estimated that she and her navigator had traveled about 22,000 miles (in forty days) and had about 7,000 to go. She yearned now for familiar faces and beloved places— home in Rye most of all—and would be glad to close the book on the more adventurous phase of her life. She was determined to be home for the Fourth of July and well in advance of any celebrations of her thirty-ninth birthday. "Whether everything to be done can be done within this time limit," she wrote in her log, "remains to be seen."

It had taken Amelia and Noonan almost eight hours, fighting head winds all the way, to fly from Port Darwin to Lae, New Guinea. There had been a two-day stopover at Port Darwin, unexplained in Amelia's log or the account for the newspaper syndicate; perhaps both she and Noonan had needed the rest. Once they reached Lae—the jumpoff for Howland Island, the second to last scheduled stop before reaching Oakland, California—there would be no time for rest; they would have to take off the moment weather conditions were favorable.

To reach Lae they had to traverse the Arufa Sea, Torres Strait, and Gulf of Papua—1,200 miles, mostly over water, through low-hanging clouds. Menacing though they were in a sense, the cloud formations were gorgeous. They climbed into what Amelia called "fairy-story sky country" to clear the New Guinea mountains. Even at 11,000 feet the sky was "peopled with grotesque cloud creatures who eyed us with ancient wisdom as we threaded our way through its white shining valleys."

There were adequate landing and servicing facilities

below—a strip hacked out of the jungle, 3,000 feet long, ending at a cliff overhanging the waters of the gulf. When they landed, they even found hangar space for the Electra.

Amelia and her navigator went to a newly built hotel in Lae after being driven into town past settlements of thatched native huts built on pilings and hanging out over the water. Late on the day of their arrival, June 30, they were hopeful of taking off the next morning for Howland Island. "Tomorrow," Amelia wrote, "we should be rolling down the runway, bound for points east. . . . If not, we cannot be home by the Fourth of July as we had hoped, even though we are one day up on the calendar of California. It is Wednesday here, but Tuesday there. On this next hop we cross the 180th Meridian, the international dateline when clocks turn back twenty-four hours."

The next day, July 1, they learned that despite their eagerness to be on their way, they would not be able to take off. The Electra had been loaded to capacity with gasoline and oil for the 2,556-mile jump to the central Pacific. The weather experts, however, advised against a takeoff; the wind was blowing the wrong way and clouds were piling up, and it was felt that they should wait for the most favorable conditions.

Also—and more ominously than Amelia gave any hint in her last transmissions to the United States—Noonan was having instrument troubles. He was "unable, because of radio difficulties, to set his chronometers. Any lack of knowledge of their fastness and slowness would defeat the accuracy of celestial navigation. Howland is such a small spot in the Pacific that every aid to locating it must be available." Noonan knew even better than Amelia how disastrous that might be and worked to calibrate his chronometers with the malfunctioning 50-watt radio set on the Electra. An error of one minute on his chronometers would put the plane four miles off course.

Amelia provided little detail on the efforts made to correct their navigational difficulties. It would almost appear from her writing that other considerations had equal weight. She mentioned the fact that during their two days at Lae they "worked very hard" repacking the plane and throwing out anything not absolutely needed.

They even took time out for sight-seeing, obtaining a truck from the manager of the hotel where they were staying and visiting a nearby native village. Amelia still had enough energy, by her own accounting, to be fascinated by the details of native life. She and Noonan were amused by the fact that the villagers trained their pigs to act as watchdogs, and "Fred said he would hate to come home late at night and admit being bitten by a pig!"

The jungle, she discovered, had a "strange fascination" for her. In the last of her writings she indicated that she was afflicted by divergent impulses. "I wish," she said, "we could stay here peacefully for a time and see something of this strange land." But her last written words were: "I shall be glad when we have the hazards of its [the Pacific's] navigation behind us."

Yet there must have been a lot more on her mind than was indicated by Amelia's sketchy account of the two days at Lae—the last two days, probably, of her life. Hitting Howland Island had always been uppermost as the most dangerous part of the venture. In the vastness of the central Pacific it was only a speck. Howland was approximately two miles long by a half-mile wide, with a maximum elevation of twenty feet. It would take dead reckoning indeed, a lot of luck with the navigation, and perfectly functioning equipment to make that landfall. And with the comparatively weak signals which could be broadcast by civilian aircraft radios, they would have to home on those transmitted by the Coast Guard cutter *Itasca,* which had been stationed at Howland for that purpose. Amelia's own account of those last days on Lae, which do not even mention the *Itasca,* is more revealing for its omissions, perhaps, than for what it said.

A cloak-and-daggerish atmosphere long since has

enveloped the events preceding her takeoff, but it is clear that the United States government, particularly its armed services, had a strong vested interest in her Pacific flight.

The United States obviously, even in mid-1937, had to be seriously concerned with the possibility of war with Japan. Various military and naval prophets had been warning of the eventuality for forty years, since the surprising Japanese victory over czarist Russia. In any military and naval contest for the Pacific, the United States had been placed at a disadvantage by terms of the World War I peace treaties. Japan had received under mandate of the League of Nations most of Micronesia—the Mariana, Caroline, and Marshall island groups formerly administered by Germany. Japan was forbidden to fortify them or prepare them for any military use but had proceeded to do so, and to keep out all non-Japanese, since the early 1920's. And the Mandated Islands presented a serious threat to American positions, from the Philippines to Hawaii, in the Pacific. Japan now controlled the Pacific islands north of the equator with the exception of Midway, Guam, and Wake.

To counteract the increasing Japanese military and naval strength in Micronesia, particularly in the Marshalls, the United States needed an advance air base on

Howland, which would place the more modern bombers within range of the Marshalls and the huge, closely guarded Japanese naval base at Truk. But there was a stumbling block: Howland was under the jurisdiction of the Department of the Interior, and Ernest Gruening, who supervised administration of island territories, decided his budget would not cover the construction of an airfield. President Roosevelt and his military advisers got around that when Amelia, at the urging of Air Corps officers, asked for permission to refuel at Howland instead of Midway, which could be done only if landing facilities were built on Howland. That would have to be done on a crash basis. A Presidential order was issued for the work to be done early in 1937. The Air Corps was delighted because it would have facilities for land-based reconnaissance and bombing planes. Furthermore Amelia Earhart's flight, if it was successful, would prove the feasibility of Air Corps operations over the Pacific and encourage the development of long-range aircraft: the Flying Fortresses and Super Fortresses to come. Later, when the time for reflection and recrimination arrived, there were many who believed that the whole round-the-world flight was a military setup; that secret funds had been provided for the purchase of Amelia's new plane; that the concealed purpose of her flight was the construction of a Howland base from which the Japanese forward bases could be pulverized from the air.

Certainly the United States military had long been obsessed with the strategic strength of the Japanese in that part of the Pacific world. The Army Air Corps was deeply concerned by the Mandated Islands, and the leading pioneer of military aviation, General Billy Mitchell, made a tour around the area late in 1923. As a young officer Mitchell had served in the Philippines and absorbed the conviction of most Old Asia Hands that sooner or later Japan would attack United States possessions without warning. His survey of what the Japanese were doing in their protectorate of Micronesia concluded with the prediction that the Japanese would use those islands as forward bases for an attack on Pearl Harbor. Furthermore, with bull's-eye accuracy, he forecast that the surprise attack would be launched on a Sunday morning.

With all their suspicions of what the Japanese were doing in the Marianas, the Carolines, and the Marshalls, United States intelligence officers could prove nothing because Japan refused permission for any foreign ships to enter the Micronesian harbors, and only a few visitors from other countries were allowed to venture there. The League of Nations, weakened by a long sequence of blows to its prestige, was powerless to enforce the provision of the mandate that "no military or naval bases shall be established, or fortifications erected in the territory."

The Carolines, the Marianas, and the Marshalls were closed off; overflights, innocent or otherwise, would be confronted by swarming Zeros, and visitors dropping in from the sky, accidentally or not, would be met with, at best, a cold hostility.

Undoubtedly Amelia had been briefed on most aspects of the western Pacific situation. At least she knew they could not afford to veer very far north of the equator, except over the British-held Gilbert Islands almost due east of Howland. (One odd circumstance was that the British authorities on the Gilberts were not alerted to give her radio assistance.) That last day on Lae she and Fred Noonan must have spent anxious hours over their flight plan. They not only had to find Howland but avoid the Japanese Mandated Islands. If they had any other mission to make than landfall, and there is no absolute proof that they did, that was just one more thing to worry about.

CHAPTER 17

FLYING INTO YESTERDAY

THE LAST PEOPLE KNOWN TO HAVE SEEN Amelia Earhart and Fred Noonan are those who gathered on the airfield outside Lae to watch their Electra take off, zoom upward from the cliffs overhanging the Huon Gulf, and rapidly become a glint of bright metal on the horizon and then disappear. It was July 2 in Lae, July 1 on Howland. Since the international dateline lay across their flight path, they were flying into yesterday; or put another way, they were gaining a day. Not that it mattered in their case. Their lives were now measured in hours.

They took off with a plane fully loaded with 1,150 gallons of gasoline, enough to carry them 4,000 miles if they didn't run into storms or strong head winds: more than enough to reach Howland even if they had some difficulty with weather or navigation. The island was so small they could not rely on dead reckoning. It was up to Fred Noonan to guide them to their next destination. And that depended to some extent on the weather: It would have to be unclouded for Noonan to take his fixes on the sun by day and the stars by night. Once they were more than 500 miles out they would not be able to stay in radio contact with Lae.

Communication with Lae, as well as the Coast Guard direction finder up ahead, was ruled out by the fact that in Miami Amelia had ordered a 250-foot wire trailing antenna removed; she believed it would be too much trouble to play out and reel in the antenna during a flight. Yet Paul Mantz had insisted on its installation, and his forebodings about the success of the flight had only increased when he heard the news from Miami. Her radio equipment worked well in voice communication, Mantz had been advised by other experts, but it had serious shortcomings as a navigational aid; it wasn't high-powered enough to enable ground stations or ships at sea to take a fix on the plane.

Mantz had gone to the trouble of asking the manufacturer, Western Electric, how to boost the equipment's capabilities. According to Mantz's biographer, Don Dwiggins, a Western Electric executive had wired back:

"To obtain satisfactory results on 500 kilocycles, a trailing wire at least 250 feet long should be used."

Mantz did not see how Amelia could home in on Howland Island, on the most perilous leg of her flight, without the trailing antenna he had installed. He was both enraged at the way his expertise had been ignored and fearful for Amelia's safety.

According to Amelia's flight plan, the Electra would be within radio range of Howland around daybreak. At Howland the Coast Guard cutter *Itasca* would be waiting to send homing signals (which, of course, Amelia wouldn't be able to receive). On the island itself a new high-frequency direction finder of the most advanced design had been installed as an additional aid. But somehow, apparently because of a lack of coordination between the group on Howland and her own flight headquarters, she had not been informed of the direction finder.

There were two other American ships detailed to offer assistance if necessary. The USS *Swan* was stationed halfway between Howland and Hawaii in case Amelia overshot Howland. The USS *Ontario* was on patrol between Lae and Howland.

The Electra took off at 10:30 A.M. It didn't have too

much runway, considering the fact that the 3,000-foot strip hacked out of the New Guinea jungle ended abruptly at cliffs, with the sea far below. It was a struggle getting the heavily loaded plane into the air. But Amelia lifted off with 150 feet of runway to spare.

From then on, all that is known of the flight consists of fragmentary, static-blurred messages, except for the first transmission, which was clear enough. Amelia's call letters were KHAQQ. It was arranged that she would transmit her call signal and any other flight information at a quarter after and a quarter to each hour. The *Itasca* would send homing signals and weather reports on the hour and the half hour.

At 5:20 P.M. (Lae time) the New Guinea station received a message from Amelia giving her position, 795 miles from Lae, on course and not far from the Solomons. No trouble was reported, though she and Noonan were believed to have encountered strong headwinds along the way.

On the *Itasca* the long watch had begun. In the communications center Chief Radioman Leo G. Bellarts was standing by at the two receivers and transmitter. Two other men were on duty with the ship's direction finder and the high-frequency model ashore. Also in the radio room on the cutter were Commander W. K. Thompson, the *Itasca*'s captain; other officers and enlisted men; Richard B. Black, the field representative of the Interior Department; and correspondents for the Associated Press and United Press.

All through the night these men stood by the loudspeaker in the radio shack straining their ears for Amelia's signals.

The rest of Amelia Earhart's story—the verifiable details—is told in the log of the *Itasca*.

Every hour and half hour its transmitter sent out weather reports and the homing signals. At 12:15 A.M. the *Itasca* sent a message to the cutter *Ontario* asking if it had heard the Electra's signal, but it hadn't. At 1:15 the *Itasca* still hadn't heard from Amelia, but there was no alarm aboard the Coast Guard cutter because it was reckoned that she must be at least a thousand miles off Howland. Ten minutes later the *Itasca* radioed Amelia, advising her that no transmissions had been received from her and requesting that she "please observe schedules with key." There was no answer.

The first fragmentary signal from the Electra came through heavy static at 2:45 A.M. Not much could be learned from that transmission, except for the encouraging fact that they were in contact. The newspaper correspondents listening at the loudspeaker later reported that they could make out Amelia's voice reporting, calmly enough, "Cloudy and overcast," but static drowned out the rest of her words.

On receiving that first message, knowing that maintaining contact might be difficult because of weather conditions, the *Itasca* broadcast to all stations in the Pacific a request that they check whether the cutter's signals were being received. The *Itasca* was heard clearly enough throughout the area. It was Amelia's transmissions that were weak and indistinct.

At 3 A.M. the *Itasca* transmitted the weather report—clear skies, calm seas, ceiling unlimited, east wind at 8 miles per hour—both by voice and key. The cutter then began sending out the homing signal, the letter *A,* which was supposed to bring the Electra through the dawn skies toward a safe landing on Howland.

At 3:30 the *Itasca,* by voice, requested Amelia to give her position and her estimated time of arrival on her next scheduled transmission at 3:45 A.M.

Amelia's voice was heard on schedule: "*Itasca* from Earhart . . . *Itasca* from Earhart. . . . Overcast. . . . Will listen on hour and half hour on 3,105 [kilocycles, her designated frequency]. . . . Will listen on hour and half hour on 3,105. . . ."

The *Itasca* then repeated the request for her position and estimated time of arrival, but there was no reply.

Nothing further was heard from the Electra between 3:45 A.M. and 6:15 A.M. At that point Amelia had been airborne for almost eighteen hours; her fuel supply would last about four more hours. She asked for a bearing on 3,105 kilocycles on the hour, would whistle into her microphone so the *Itasca*'s direction finder could get a fix on her position. She added that she was "about two hundred miles out and no landfall."

Half an hour later, at 6:45, Amelia's voice came over the loudspeaker in the *Itasca* radio shack quite clearly and with an unmistakable urgency:

"Please take a bearing on us, and report in half hour. I will make a noise in microphone. About one hundred miles out."

The transmission was too brief, however, for the high-frequency direction finder ashore to get a bearing on her. From then until 7:42 the *Itasca* kept sending her messages asking that she reply on the designated frequency and sending the homing signal.

Then Amelia's voice broke into the tense silence of the *Itasca*'s radio room not at her scheduled time of 7:45 but three minutes earlier. Those who heard it said her voice was high-pitched, edged by alarm:

"We must be on you. But cannot see you. But gas is running low. Been unable to reach you by radio. We are flying at altitude one thousand feet."

That was a rather low altitude for a plane searching for landfall in what, around Howland, was good visibility.

The *Itasca* kept pleading with her to acknowledge its messages, but it was apparent that the radio on the Electra was neither receiving nor sending in reliable fashion.

From Amelia's next transmission at 7:58 A.M. it seemed that she and Noonan believed they had arrived in the Howland area. "We are circling," she advised the cutter, "but cannot hear you. Go ahead on 7,500 [kilocycles] either now or on schedule time of half hour."

The *Itasca* immediately began sending her the homing signal without interruption.

From 7:58 to 8:45 nothing more was heard from the Electra, though the *Itasca* urgently radioed Amelia at 8:33, "Will you please come in and answer on 3,105. We are transmitting constantly on 7,500 kilocycles. We do not hear you on 3,105. Please answer on 3,105. Go ahead."

By then the tension in the radio room of the *Itasca* was almost unbearable. The Electra's radio equipment obviously was malfunctioning, and if Amelia couldn't lock in on the *Itasca*'s homing signals, it would take sheer luck to bring her in safely. Noonan, it would seem, had been unable to continue celestial navigation because of the "cloudy and overcast" conditions Amelia had reported during the night. And the plane's gasoline supply would last only another hour or so. There was no way of knowing whether Amelia, at last report, was really only 100 miles off Howland, as she believed.

The 8:45 transmission from the Electra was anything but reassuring. Amelia's voice was strained with anxiety as she reported: "We are on a line of position 157 [degrees] —337 [degrees]. Will repeat this message on 6,210 kilocycles. Wait, listening on 6,210 kilocycles. We are running north and south."

To this the *Itasca* immediately replied: "We heard you OK on 3,105 kilocycles. Please stay on 3,105. Do not hear you on 6,210. Maintain QSO on 3,105."

The *Itasca* kept urging Amelia to reply on her assigned frequency.

For the next hour, until 10 A.M., the *Itasca*'s radio mast continued crackling with urgent pleas to Amelia to come in on her frequency, to give her position, to maintain contact as best she could.

But the loudspeaker amplifying any transmissions from the plane was silent. It stayed silent as the hands of the clock passed 10 A.M.—the time when it had to be presumed the Electra would be running out of fuel, though Amelia might have more flying time, possibly until noon, if she rigorously conserved her gasoline.

At 10 A.M. a feeling of doom began to settle on the men crowded into the *Itasca*'s radio shack. There was a glimmering of hope, but no more, that if Amelia was circling north of Howland, she might be able to land on one of the British-protected Gilbert Islands.

CHAPTER 18

"FIND AMELIA EARHART"

WITHIN FIFTEEN MINUTES OF THE TIME when it was presumed Amelia Earhart's plane was exhausting its fuel supply, the largest sea search in the history of the U.S. Navy was begun, and it gathered force and numbers in the next several days. The *Itasca* led off at 10:15 A.M. July 2 (Howland time) by steaming at flank speed toward the northwest. Commander Thompson had to make a quick decision on where to begin his sweep of thousands of square miles of ocean and had slender evidence on which to base it. Amelia's only position report had been "We are on a line of position 157–337," but no reference point was given. The *Itasca's* only hope was to start searching in the northwest quadrant indicated by the 337-degree reference. If she had wandered slightly off course to the south in her attempt to obtain a sighting of Howland, she could have landed at Baker Island, 38 miles south of Howland.

The *Itasca* continued transmitting to the Electra even as she steamed northwest at top speed. There was a possibility that even if the Electra was down, she could be kept afloat for a while and Noonan might get the radio in better working order. There was also a possibility she might have ditched just off one of the Gilberts, in which case she might not be heard from for days. There was even a possibility, not a pleasant one, that she might have had to land at or near one of the Japanese-held Marshall or Caroline islands.

Later that day the Navy dispatched a long-distance reconnaissance plane from Pearl Harbor piloted by Commander Warren W. Harvey to join the search in the Howland area. The next morning the commandant of the 14th Naval District, with headquarters at Pearl Harbor, forwarded a message from Commander Harvey to Commander Thompson on the *Itasca:* "About 420 miles north of Howland. Last two hours in extremely bad weather between altitude 2,000 feet and 12,000 feet. Snow sleet rain electrical storms. In daylight conditions look equally bad. Cloud tops appear to be 18,000 feet or more. Am returning to Pearl Harbor. Now have 900 gallons of fuel on board."

It was probable that Amelia's plane had run into the

same violent and widespread storm. With clouds extending up to the 18,000-foot level, she would have been unable to fly high enough for Fred Noonan to shoot star sights and obtain a fix on their position.

In Washington President Roosevelt ordered the Navy to use all available men and ships and planes to join in the search as soon as possible. Aside from the fact that the President and Mrs. Roosevelt were personal friends of Amelia and her husband, Roosevelt must have felt a degree of personal responsibility for whatever might have happened to Amelia. The designation of Howland as her first stop in the central Pacific, instead of Midway, had been engineered by executive order, which directed the construction of landing facilities on Howland. The Navy Department immediately forwarded the order of the Chief of Naval Operations, Admiral William D. Leahy, for a search of the 250,000 square miles of central Pacific by an aircraft carrier, a battleship, four destroyers, and a minesweeper.

The night of July 3 the carrier *Lexington* was docked at Santa Barbara, California, preparing for a Fourth of July reception for civilians. Instead, it weighed anchor and headed out to sea, to be joined en route by three destroyers, the *Drayton,* the *Lamson,* and the *Cushing.*

The *Lexington* contingent did not reach the search

area until July 13, upon which, shortly after dawn, it launched sixty planes to hunt for Amelia and Noonan west and east of Howland Island. In the next five days the carrier's planes searched an area of 151,000 square miles.

The *Lexington* task force conducted an intensive search of a 120-mile radius around Howland and including the Gilbert Islands. In a subsequent report of his actions—all of which had negative results as far as turning up the missing Electra or its occupants—Captain Leigh Noyes of the *Lexington* came to certain conclusions which he summarized as follows:

> *The information actually available indicated that the plane arrived in the vicinity of Howland Island at about eight o'clock in the morning of 2 July. During the night run the navigator should have been able to check his position accurately and frequently by star sights, and it must be assumed that this was done, and that the navigator knew the position of his plane and the ground speed it had been making through the night.* [This, of course, did not take into account the storm reported by Commander Harvey on his search by seaplane out of Pearl Harbor or Amelia's own report that they were flying through overcast skies.] *Information available on the weather conditions do not indicate that any radical change in direction or force of the*

wind occurred at Howland Island during the two and one-half hours preceding eight o'clock.

At 0615 the plane reported that they were 200 miles out; one hour and forty-five minutes later they circled and attempted to pick up the island. This time agrees very well with the time it would take the plane to cover 200 miles at 111 knots, and it also checked with the time at which the Itasca *reported hearing the plane's radio at its greatest strength. All of the above indicates that the plane's 0615 position was reasonably accurate.*

This being the case, it is not reasonable to suppose that the plane was more than sixty miles off its course one hour and forty-five minutes later. Having arrived at the navigator's position of the island the plane maneuvered to make a landfall, circling first, and then running north and south indicating they were fairly sure of their longitude. With the gasoline supply practically exhausted . . . it is not likely the plane ventured more than forty miles from the navigator's best position. Assuming that the gasoline gave out when the plane was at the end of one of these runs farthest from the island, the distance from Howland would be only 100 miles.

Captain Noyes' report raised one most significant point—that Amelia's transmissions came through loud and clear twice in the several hours before silence fell, indicating she was quite close to Howland, as she believed.

While the air and sea search was being pressed, the Lockheed engineers who were responsible for the design and construction of the Electra were sought out and interviewed on the possibility that Amelia and her navigator might survive a forced landing at sea. The Electra's empty tanks would keep her afloat, they estimated, for nine hours at the most. But her radio could not operate with the plane on the sea because it was powered by the right engine.

George Putnam had been waiting in San Francisco to greet Amelia when she landed at the Oakland airport and completed her round-the-world flight. His last talk with her had been over the shortwave radio from Karachi, when he was still in New York. Their last exchange, recorded by a dictaphone in the New York *Herald Tribune* office, had been Putnam's query, "Is everything about the ship okay now?"

"Yes," Amelia had replied.

"Good night, hon."

"Good night. I'll be sitting in Oakland waiting for you."

Putnam was stunned by the news flash that Amelia

was missing and shocked by succeeding bulletins that she might not survive a forced landing at sea. He always had as much confidence in Amelia's ability to fly through anything as she had in herself—perhaps more, because she understood more completely the chanciness of every phase of her calling.

His first action was to send a radiogram to the naval search headquarters at Pearl Harbor: "If they are down, they can stay afloat indefinitely. Their empty tanks will give them buoyancy. Besides, they have all the emergency equipment they'll need—everything." By everything, he meant a life raft and some emergency rations.

Even with his confidence in Amelia's survival quotient, he knew that they would have to be rescued quickly, perhaps in a matter of hours, especially if she or Noonan had been injured in a rough landing, certainly within days.

The more orthodox search went on day after day, with naval vessels and carrier planes crisscrossing the waters of the central Pacific (but taking care not to stray into Japanese air space or coastal areas in the Mandated Islands) and smaller ships calling at every island and combing every coral reef for some evidence of what had happened to the Electra and its occupants. Two privately owned vessels were chartered to cruise as far south as Gardner Island and the Phoenix Islands, British possessions, north to Christmas and Fanning islands, and then to the west.

What they were looking for now, two weeks after the plane presumably had gone down, was the wreckage of the Electra; the possibility that Amelia and her companion could have survived on some tiny island or on their life raft was dim indeed. There was also some hope that they either had landed on one of the Japanese islands or had been picked up by one of the ubiquitous Japanese fishing vessels that plied those waters, but it never materialized. The Japanese said they knew nothing of the termination of Amelia's flight.

There was great pressure on the Navy, of course, to come up with some answer to the riddle of the Electra's disappearance. The press and public, both in the States and around the world, clamored for a solution to the mystery.

The Coast Guard cutter *Itasca,* while combing the Gilberts, sent an officer ashore at Tarawa, the British administrative headquarters, to confer with the British Resident, who expressed surprise that the two radio stations in those islands had not been informed of Amelia's flight and asked to help in its navigation. Neither of the stations had picked up her messages, fragmentary as they were, while she was approaching Howland. Yet her course lay only 20 miles south of the southernmost of the Gilberts.

A widespread and intense radio watch was maintained throughout the search period in the faint hope that if the missing fliers had reached some deserted island or coral reef they might be able to send a signal.

Back in Los Angeles, Paul Mantz himself believed that Amelia and her navigator had "one chance in a thousand" of having survived a crash landing at sea. Two things could have happened to them, he told reporters. "One: The navigator missed the island and Miss Earhart flew until out of gas, and due to fatigue tried to land too high over the clear water which would result in the ship 'falling off,' causing a crash that would kill them instantly. Two: If the sea were very rough, it would be quite hard to judge the distance properly, thus causing her to fly into a heavy roller, having a similar result."

By late in July the whole area, with the Japanese-controlled areas excepted, had been searched, and not one sure clue to the disappearance had been found. The failure was dramatically symbolized for the American people when the *Lexington*, its fuel and other supplies exhausted by a fifteen-day effort, steamed through the

Golden Gate. As the carrier plowed into San Francisco Bay it lowered its colors to half-mast in tribute to the lost fliers.

Lost—but not forgotten.

Already the speculation, much of it necessarily ill-informed, had begun and would intensify.

The public was not satisfied to be left with a mystery. It seemed an indignity, somehow, that the life of Amelia Earhart, then undoubtedly the most heroic and inspiring figure of American womanhood, should be closed in such a manner. Where no ending of indubitable authenticity could be supplied for her life, no suitable conclusion for her legend arrived at, the public imagination would take over. Amelia Earhart, once a living woman, had become a part of American mythology.

CHAPTER 19

NO END TO THE MYSTERY

ALMOST INEVITABLY THE DEATH OF A FAMOUS or notorious person arouses a whirlwind of speculation. The ordinary fact of death is somehow unacceptable. The rumor factory works on a round-the-clock schedule. Various investigators, largely self-nominated, rush into print with their theories and find an eager audience.

In the case of Amelia Earhart, the speculation was greatly enhanced by the close-mouthed attitude of the federal bureaucracy, a seeming reluctance by the Navy, in particular, to be entirely frank about what it learned, and the State Department's traditionally guarded approach to anything that might cause friction with another nation, even a recent enemy.

The favorite theory—and it has not been diminished by

the years—is that Amelia Earhart and Fred Noonan were captured by the Japanese, probably because they had secretly undertaken a mission from naval intelligence to spy on Japanese fortification of their Mandated Islands, and that subsequently they were executed. To those who like an admixture of melodrama with their history, that seems to be a satisfactory explanation of what happened to them. It supplies a heroic ending, much more glamorous than the possibility that their plane simply ran out of gasoline and went into the drink.

Yet those most intimately connected with Amelia Earhart, those most familiar with her career, were unanimously inclined to reject such solutions to what others regarded as a mystery. "To produce a sensational denouement for Amelia's story," as her sister, Muriel, has written, "recent biographers have mingled hearsay and possibility and have irresponsibly called it probability." As far as her family was concerned, "the manner of Amelia's death is not of great moment. . . . That she did not live to have a child of her own and enjoy the honors she earned is sad."

Amelia's contemporaries in the pioneering of aviation, familiar as they were with the hazards she faced in that time of uncertain navigational aids and rudimentary radio transmissions, concluded that she simply lost out in the greatest gamble of her life. "For months and years," wrote Ruth Nichols in *Wings for Life,* "her friends and family clung to the forlorn hope that somewhere, somehow, she might still be alive, that once again they would see that cropped golden head and that boyish grin, hear that gay voice and grasp that strong, slender hand. But after almost twenty years have passed, I feel now as I did then—that Amelia flew on across the trackless Pacific until her last drop of fuel was gone and then sank quickly and cleanly into the deep blue sea." It was enough for her that Amelia would "live on in memory as young, golden and unafraid."

After the war ended, the Navy Department, confronted by so many rumors that it *knew* what had happened to Amelia, officially declared that the disappearance was still a mystery; that she had not been on a mission for any branch of the United States government; that it had no evidence that she had been a prisoner of the Japanese or had been killed by them.

So the story of her life ends with a probably insoluble mystery, an unsatisfactory conclusion to one of the most remarkable American lives. The manner of her death, as her family and friends insisted, is no longer of paramount importance. The real tragedy, as newspaper columnist Jay Franklin wrote at the time, was that "the very qualities which brought her fame in the late 1920's are no longer needed by the late 1930's. A single decade has brought such changes in aviation that chance and guess-work have been largely eliminated. The future lies with the undramatic experts who bring the planes in on time, safely. The romantic whoopla artists have outstayed their aeronautical welcome, and the individual once more becomes submerged in the organization."

It was also noted at the time of her death that she disappeared just when Pan American and Imperial Airways were establishing a routine round-the-world air service. "One plane missing," as a newspaper editorial on her disappearance remarked, "far out on the lonely Pacific. Another plane heading into the dawn, half a world away. And the day of the ocean pioneers is closed."

Amelia Earhart herself recognized that her last flight closed an era and unavailingly hoped to go into a graceful retirement. It was her thirty-nine years, not the moment of her death, that counted. Those years are a continuing inspiration to all who believe in humanity's ability to surpass itself, to reach for the stars.

Amelia Earhart Timeline

July 24, 1897: Born in Atchison, Kansas. Amelia Mary was named after her two grandmothers.

1915: Graduated on time from Hyde Park High School in Chicago, despite having attended six high schools.

1918: Became a nurse's aide at Spadina Military Hospital in Toronto, Canada.

1920: Took her first airplane ride.

January 3, 1921: Began flying lessons with Neta Snook.

May 16, 1922: Received pilot's license.

July 1921: Bought first plane, a Kinner Airster (Canary).

October 22, 1922: Broke women's altitude record when she rose to 14,000 feet.

1922: Sold her plane and purchased a 1922 Kissel Goldbug touring car which she nicknamed "Yellow Peril."

June 17–18, 1928: First woman to fly across the Atlantic; 20 hours 40 minutes (Fokker F7, *Friendship).*

Summer 1928: Bought an Avro Avian Moth, a small English plane famous because Lady Mary Heath, Britain's foremost woman pilot had flown it solo from Capetown, South Africa to London.

Fall 1928: Published her book *20 Hours 40 Minutes,* toured and lectured; became aviation editor of Cosmopolitan magazine.

August 1929: Placed third in the First Women's Air Derby, nicknamed the Powder Puff Derby; upgraded from her Avian to a Lockheed Vega.

June 25, 1930: Set women's speed record for 100 kilometers with no load, and with a load of 500 kilograms.

July 5, 1930: Set speed record for of 181.18mph over a 3 kilometer course.

February 7, 1931: Married George Putnam.

April 8, 1931: Set woman's autogiro altitude record with 18,415 feet in a Pitcairn autogiro, an early helicopter.

May 20–21, 1932: First woman to fly solo across the Atlantic, 14 hours 56 minutes (it was also the 5th anniversary of Lindberg's Atlantic flight); awarded National Geographic Society's gold medal from President Herbert Hoover; Congress awarded her the Distinguished Flying Cross; wrote *For The Fun of It* about her journey.

August 24–25, 1932: First woman to fly solo nonstop coast to coast; set women's nonstop transcontinental speed record, flying 2,447.8 miles in 19 hours 5minutes.

Fall 1932: Elected president of the Ninety Nines, a new women's aviation club that she helped to form.

September 1, 1935: Joined the faculty of Purdue University as a career consultant to women students.

January 11, 1935: First person to solo the 2,408-mile distance across the Pacific between Honolulu and Oakland, California; also first flight where a civilian aircraft carried a two-way radio.

April 19-20, 1935: First person to fly solo from Los Angeles to Mexico City; 13hours 23 minutes.

May 8, 1935: First person to fly solo nonstop from Mexico City to Newark; 14 hours 19 minutes.

June 1, 1937: Began flight around the world June 1937; first person to fly from the Red Sea to India.

July 1937: Reported missing en route to Howland Island in the Pacific Ocean.

Aerial Records Set by Amelia Earhart

June 17, 1928: First woman to fly across the Atlantic as a passenger.

April 8, 1931: Altitude record for autogiros, 18,451 feet.

May 20–21, 1932: First woman to fly solo across the Atlantic.

August 24–25, 1932: Women's nonstop transcontinental speed record, Los Angeles to Newark, 19 hours, 5 minutes.

July 7–8, 1933: Broke her own transcontinental speed record, Los Angeles to Newark, 17 hours, 7 minutes.

January 11–12, 1935: First to solo from Honolulu to mainland (Oakland).

April 19–20, 1935: First to solo from Los Angeles to Mexico City.

May 8, 1935: First to solo from Mexico City to Newark.

June–July, 1937: First to fly around the world at the equator (not completed).

Index

Bibliography

The principal published sources for this book were:

Balchen, Bernt, *Come North with Me*. New York, 1958.

Byrd, Richard E., *Skyward*. New York, 1928.

Cochran, Jacqueline, *The Stars at Noon*. Boston, 1954.

Earhart, Amelia, *Last Flight* (edited by George Palmer Putnam). New York, 1937.

—— *The Fun of It*. New York, 1932.

—— *20 hrs., 40 min.* New York, 1928.

Goerner, Fred, *The Search for Amelia Earhart*. New York, 1966.

Lindbergh, Charles A., *The Spirit of St. Louis*. New York, 1953.

Morrissey, Muriel Earhart, *Courage Is the Price*. Wichita, 1963.

Nichols, Ruth, *Wings for Life*. Philadelphia, 1958.

Putnam, George Palmer, *Soaring Wings*. New York, 1939.
—— *Wide Margins*. New York, 1942.
Railey, Hilton H., *Touch'd with Madness*. New York, 1938.
Rickenbacker, Eddie, *Rickenbacker*. New York, 1967.
Thaden, Louise, *High, Wide and Frightened*. New York, 1938.

ABOUT THE AUTHOR

John Burke started out as a reporter who wrote for newspapers in cities across the United States. He decided to concentrate on writing magazine articles and books about Americans past and present. He is the author of over fifty books—novels, biographies, and histories. He spent much of his writing career commuting between two places he loved very much—Maine and Ireland. John Burke was a pseudonym for his real name, Richard O'Connor.

BOOKS IN THIS SERIES

★ STERLING POINT BOOKS